Anchored in the Storm

Pursuing Christ in the Midst of Life's Trials

ADAM HOLLAND

ISBN: 1532976623
ISBN-13: 978-1532976629

To the weak and weary in this world, may you see Jesus Christ as your strength and life, and may you be anchored in His Word, and by the presence of His saints during your storm.

CONTENTS

FOREWORD

*"But he knows the way that I take; when he has tried me,
I shall come out as gold" ~Job 23:10*

Let's face it, nobody registers for the school of suffering. But suffering may be the best educator of the soul. As a pastor—one who shepherds people—I find myself sitting in the front of the classroom, seeing firsthand the schooling that suffering wreaks on an individual or family.

Why God allows pain and suffering is a most difficult question. Why is there pain and suffering? How can we live through pain? Is there really hope? How could we ever get over the loss of someone we love? Why does Christianity offer the right and best answers? Adam Holland doesn't duck the hard question, but his answers are found in his journey.

The problem of evil is the most demanding question that we face intellectually. Derek Thomas, for instance, says this is the most troubling and perplexing question we ever face. John Stott adds, "The fact of suffering undoubtedly constitutes the single greatest challenge to the Christian faith."

It was a Monday night, and my wife and I got one of those calls—that the doctor found a mass in Adam's brain that looked like cancer. As we prayed with his family and him that first night, you could see this was a course they would never choose for themselves. But that night the bell rang, and the class began. And now in Adam Holland's book on his education during a season of suffering, it is a journey that takes the reader as close to the fire as anyone can get. It is personal; it is raw; and it is Christ exalting.

In my own journey to understand the reason for suffering, I found that the answer is found not in the *why* but in the *who*. I spent almost a year going through the book of Job, looking to find this elusive answer to why God allows suffering. In forty-two chapters, with lots of words, there was no answer to why Job was to suffer. Yet God was not silent; He said to Job, "Look at who I am." God asked Job—and Adam Holland—to trust the Sovereign *who*.

1

This book reminds us of our great High Priest, who can sympathize with our suffering. Jesus is the author of faith because he holds the key to trusting the who—the Father. Jesus understood suffering firsthand. In the Garden of Gethsemane, Jesus saw that if he obeyed God fully, he would suffer greatly. Jesus submitted himself to the Father and came out the great victor—the who, who during suffering, is the one with you, in every class. The who, who permits suffering but takes no pleasure in suffering. The who, who says, "My ways are not your ways, so trust me."

You see, if we are to understand how to walk with God through pain and suffering, then we need to understand the very nature and character of God. Throughout the book the reader is reminded of the best news for those that enter the school of suffering: that Jesus takes every class with you.

This book is saturated with scripture, and Holland soaks the pages with majestic lyrics and poetry by godly men and women. This book could only be written by someone who has an earned Masters in suffering. Adam Holland is not only a dear friend and part of our church family; he is an example to all.

This book is about the making of gold.

Pastor Todd Smith
Crossroads Community Church
Valencia, California

TO THE READER

Life goes on day by day in the nondescript town I grew up in, currently live in, and work in as a history teacher at one of our local high schools. But ordinary lives can sometimes turn and take on extraordinary destinies.

Within my own ordinary life, the most extraordinary thing was about to happen in the spring of 2014—I got cancer.

I can not remember the exact date in the fall of 2013, but I woke up one night, and before my eyes—or so I thought—flashed familiar images, very much like deja vu. I could not process the images or what was happening. After a few minutes, I went back to sleep. When I awoke in the morning, I recalled that something had happened, but I couldn't place what had occurred that night. When I got out of bed, my whole body ached: from joints to muscles, everything hurt. For the next week my body continued to ache. This would happen at least once a month into 2014.

On January 2, 2014, I woke up on the floor of my bedroom. On the floor around me were objects scattered from my nightstand: a glass of water, a clock, my watch, the lamp—all on the floor. I was in a haze when I woke up and knew that something was not right. I hurriedly picked up everything, tried to dry the carpet, then went back to sleep. I woke up with a vague idea of what had happened in the night—along with a mild black eye and bruised face.

Thus started the trial of—and for—my life.

I did not go to the doctor right away, it took a few more "incidences"—as my family and I would call these occurrences—to get me there. In February, I was in my classroom teaching, and in the middle of class, I went partially blind. I could not see out of the right side of each eye. I told the kids that I had a headache and went to sit at my desk, which I rarely did as a teacher. It was then I knew something was seriously wrong, and that I needed to make an appointment with the doctor.

A few weeks later I had my first doctor's appointment. Though not initially concerned, my doctor agreed to do a variety of health assessments that, even if nothing else, would provide a basic analysis of my overall health. One of the things I strongly urged the doctor to prescribe was an MRI.

In April I would have my first MRI, the first of many to come. A few days after the MRI, the doctor's office called saying that I needed another MRI, immediately. It did not make sense to me, since I thought everything was all right, but I was more curious than worried. When I left the second MRI, I asked the technician why they had wanted another one.

"Oh, they found something. Good luck!", was the worrisome answer I received.

The next day I called the doctor's office to get the results—or at least some idea as to what was going on. However, he was out of town that week and wouldn't return until the following Tuesday. The next Monday I received a voice mail from the nurse practitioner in my doctor's office stating that the brain lesion on the first MRI was also on the second MRI. The only question I had was, "What's a brain lesion?"

The doctor called me upon his return (in the middle of my teaching day) and told me that it was a brain tumor about three inches deep into the brain—about the size of a Ping-Pong ball or silver dollar. Though concerned, he said he was confident that it was benign, based on the characteristics of the tumor.

He arranged an appointment for me to see a neurosurgeon that afternoon.

The meeting with the neurosurgeon was very informative, especially because I would have to learn an entirely new vocabulary. He didn't seem concerned, but wanted to look into it further. They scheduled yet another MRI to look directly at the tumor in order to confirm that it was benign. The Lord blessed me through all this with a neurosurgeon who was one of the top neurosurgeons in the country.

I had the MRI and over the next few days would research, along with my family, the various procedures that might be done to remove the benign tumor and restore my health. While it was a hard week, we felt that everything would be okay, and that life was somewhat under control. We prayed about the journey ahead and were confident that this would be a mere bump in the road of life.

When we met with the neurosurgeon the next week, we brought a long list of questions related to a benign tumor. He came into the room, and my parents and I were told that it was a malignant tumor.

I had cancer.

There we sat, stunned by what we heard. The conversation for that day was done. There were no questions to ask—just shock. We arranged the next appointment, leaving the office in silence and with tears building in our eyes. That night my pastor, Todd Smith, his wife, and two close family friends came over to my parents' house to sit, try to process what we had heard, and to pray. We knew the journey was going to be hard, but we didn't know how hard the road ahead would be.

The next step was to have a PET/CT scan to see if the cancer was anywhere else. Thankfully, this was an easy procedure compared to what I would face in the coming weeks. The scan revealed a mass in my lung. Again, I was unprepared to hear that news and still very naïve and ignorant about the whole thing, which raised a new set of questions for the next steps.

The good news about the lung mass was that it was easier to access than the brain tumor, and most likely, the two tumors were related. I underwent a biopsy of the lung tumor. It was a fairly easy procedure for me until the biopsy was completed. As I was moving from the biopsy table to the wheelchair, I collapsed, completely blacking out. I awoke back on the table, with the doctor and nurses inserting a valve into my chest to restore the air pressure around the lung. They told me that my right lung had collapsed, and that I could live a long life with just one lung.

The biopsy did not reveal cancer, a blessing and yet, it did not answer the question of the lung mass. It was a mystery, but we had to put that aside for a while. (It was later diagnosed as acute pneumonia. Another surprise, but I *did* get to keep my lung.)

So we returned to focusing on the brain cancer. The only option I had was to have it biopsied, which I did in June, the day after I finished teaching for the school year. No surgery is ever easy, but brain surgery has its own unique features, and the possible complications can be quite drastic: including hemorrhaging, stroke, physical disabilities, and death.

All those possibilities were running through my mind as I entered the operating room. Life on the other side of the biopsy could be entirely different.

The brain cancer biopsy surgery went well, but identifying the cancer was elusive. Initially the pathologist diagnosed it as lymphoma, which was hard for me to grasp. I knew that chemotherapy would be involved, including injecting chemo into my spinal column so that it could get to the brain tumor. This scared me more than anything.

Thankfully, a week or so later, I was informed that it was not lymphoma, but we still didn't have a final diagnosis. The only option: take the tumor out.

I sat in my living room on July 22, one day after my thirty-third birthday and one day before the brain resection (or removal of the tumor), contemplating the future, the complications of this much more delicate surgery, and the uncertain future that I might face. Life, in so many ways, had truly not gone as expected, but I trusted the plan of the Lord. A couple years prior, I had prayed for the Lord's will over my life, and I now rested in the fact that this, yes this, was His will for this time in my life.

The question was not, "Why?" As a Christ-follower, it was, "Why not?" As we prayed before the surgery the next day, I knew that whatever the outcome of the surgery, He was sovereign over my life, and there was a purpose in this storm.

The surgery went well; my neurosurgeon was confident that he got the entire tumor. It was an exciting time in the ICU that night, but this journey was not yet completed.

Once again, the cancer was very hard to diagnose. One institution said one thing, and another something different. It would not be until February 2015—and four world-renowned institutions later—that we would have a name to the type of cancer: ependymoma, graded between a two and a three, three being the highest grade of this cancer. Only around seven hundred people a year are diagnosed with this type of brain cancer. Though it was difficult to hear, it was a blessing to finally receive a true diagnosis. After its being named seven different types of cancer, we finally had one that we could focus on and research for ourselves.

After the surgery I was confronted by the truth that I would have to undergo radiation and chemotherapy.

Before starting that treatment, I had a spinal tap, where a needle was inserted into the spinal column, and spinal fluid was removed (all while I was awake) to see if there were cancer cells in the spine. The procedure was fairly easy, but the complications were another story.

If the hole in the spinal column doesn't close, the spine will leak cerebral fluid, causing one of the worst headaches imaginable—or so I was told. Over the next week a headache was building, until in the middle of one of my classes, it became intolerable. It was the worst headache I have ever had: to the point of almost throwing up and wanting to curl up in a ball on the floor and cry. I called a coworker and asked her to bring me a 7UP to calm my stomach. She did and asked if I would be okay. I told her that if I could just rest my head on my desk and tell the students what to do, I'd be fine. Thankfully, she had other plans—taking me to the nurse's office so I could lie down and planning who would take my classes for the day.

Within the next hour or so, another staff member took me to the hospital to get this resolved. The solution was very easy and very quick. They took a vial of my blood and injected it into the spinal column. This sealed the hole and stopped the leaking spinal fluid. It was miraculous, and within a half hour I felt great.

That fall, I underwent six weeks of daily radiation and chemotherapy and would continue chemotherapy throughout 2015. The six weeks of cranial radiation were very difficult, the worst being the fatigue and exhaustion that came along with having my brain radiated.

I was drained but continued teaching throughout the treatment. It was one area of normalcy for me, and though it was hard, it was well worth it. I saw the Lord's hand in allowing me to finish radiation the Friday before Thanksgiving. There was so much to be thankful for that year.

That same Thanksgiving I also celebrated the fact that I was done with chemotherapy. All three of my oncologists and my neurosurgeon agreed that continuing chemotherapy through 2015 would not be necessary.

Life had forever changed, and I could not return to the life I had before—2015 was a year of physical recovery and the beginning of a new life. Processing the cancer, coming to grips with what happened, and rebuilding my life is still underway into 2016. I am not sure if anyone can fully recover, especially knowing there is a good chance the cancer could return, and at a higher grade.

The cancer was one trial I faced in my life-- others include: family economic problems growing up, career choices right after college, extended singleness, loneliness, depression, and overall disappointment when life has not gone as expected. While I haven't faced all that a person could face in this life—and cannot say that I have experience in the trials you may face—I now understand that dealing with cancer is one of those situations in which life completely changes.

Out of my cancer came *Anchored in the Storm*, a devotional for those who are suffering. Distress and anguish in our world take on many forms, including physical, emotional, economic, and relational.

The goal of this book is to encourage and exhort your faith in Christ during the hardest, darkest, and most difficult times you may ever face.

This book is for you—so that you may know, at a deeper level, your Creator, and the glorious purposes and incredible destiny He has for you. Each entry is short so that you can focus on the verse and its encouragement—before bed, in a waiting room, before a job interview, or during the lonely times—and think about how God is working in your life. Your mind can be so clouded and distracted during these dark days that I want to give you great truths in small bites to hold on to, to relish, to mull over and pray about.

I pray that you exit your suffering stronger and closer to Christ than when you entered the trial. Think and dwell upon what is written. Pray through each entry.

I admit that I am not a pastor, theologian, or counselor, and I do not have any specific position within my church or any Christian organization. I am just like you, doing my best day by day to live my life where the Lord has placed me, striving to serve Him as best I can in His church and in my workplace, and attempting to walk beside my fellow brothers and sisters in Christ, encouraging them as we walk the path of life together.

May you be transformed.

* * *

While I was undergoing radiation and chemotherapy, my church recorded a short video of my story. I pray that it will be an encouragement to you as you weather your own storm. You may access it here:

www.anchoredinthestorm.com

SOMETHING STRANGE

"Beloved, do not be surprised at the fiery trial
when it comes upon you to test you, as though something strange
were happening to you" ~1 Peter 4:12

Did your trial come out of nowhere? Did it surprise you? It may have shocked you, but it did not shock or surprise God. He is never surprised. I pray that you can rest in that great truth.

God has every moment, every hour, and every single day under His sovereign control. The world may appear to be falling apart around you, but if you are in Christ, your world isn't falling apart. As long as Christ is in your life, your world will always remain together and won't entirely come apart, even if it feels that way. It may be shaken, but it is never destroyed. He knows exactly what He's doing in your suffering.

He knew that the trial would come at the exact moment it started. He knew the difficulties you would endure. There is nothing that surprises God. We can rest in that truth and promise.

When going through a trial, it seems like something strange and unusual is happening. There are new experiences, a new vocabulary, and new challenges to conquer. One of the blessings in your suffering is that Jesus walked all the paths that you are on—paths of suffering and darkness. He knows each step you are taking because He has taken every single step you'll ever take. You could say that He's been in your shoes. He knows each pain, each disappointment, and each heartache you have, and all He asks is that you trust and rest in Him. Through it all though, He trusted God's sovereign plan, and Jesus willingly chose suffering for your sake—for your salvation.

Christ promised that our lives were going to be hard on this earth. The gospel writer Luke states in Acts 14:22: "Through many tribulations we must enter the kingdom of God." Your present adversity allows Him to show His strength, power, and peace in your life. It allows you to shine even brighter in the darkness of this world.

Peter says that the trial is here to test you. Like the refiner's fire, this trial is testing your allegiance and faithfulness to whom and to what. Christ is taking your life and purifying it to make it more like His—just like a refiner's fire that burns away impurities from precious metals.

Are you going to trust in Christ and His Word or trust in the answers that the world provides? Are you going to hold fast to Christ, or are you going to let the world define your destiny? Is He going to be your anchor as the world falls apart, or are you going to fall apart like the world?

Whatever this world may hold against us in suffering, it should be an encouragement to us that Christ has overcome everything the world can throw at us. Truly He has overcome the world, and it holds no power over Him or His people. (*John 16:33*)

Christ is here, present in your storm.

Your next move is to decide if you are going to allow Him to work in and through your circumstances.

He's ready, are you?

REORIENT YOUR HEART

"Know that the LORD, he is God! It is he who made us, and we are his; we are his people, and the sheep of his pasture" ~ Psalm 100: 3

Part of why I write to you is to turn your eyes from your situation, away from this world, and toward God. The Psalms give us such beautiful words of encouragement and strength—far better than any modern author can do today. Of course, the source of the Psalms is He who created all things and by His sovereignty allowed all things (including pain) in this world. The Psalms are the Lord's gift of wisdom to people who find themselves in a plethora of situations. It is there for those who learn to turn their focus away from trials and celebrations, and turn to the Lord and His glory, no matter what is happening in life.

I urge you to read through every psalm over the course of your trial. Not all of the psalms will fit with your journey through the valley of suffering, but all fit with your walk with the Lord, and that matters more than anything that could happen to us—both good and bad—in this world. Many chapters were written by King David, who experienced mountaintops in joy and valleys of despair in his life, just as you are facing in yours.

During your time reading the psalms, my desire is that you will soar to the highest heights while you are in the deepest depths of your very real trial.

BE STILL AND KNOW

"Be still, and know that I am God. I will be exalted among the nations,
I will be exalted in the earth!" ~ Psalm 46:10

It is a tremendous joy to share this verse with you. It is one of those rare verses where we actually hear the voice of God. And just as the Lord spoke to the psalmist when these words were penned, the Lord is currently speaking them to you through His Word. These words are meant to calm you, help you to evaluate your heart, and give you a greater knowledge of your Lord and Savior. Imagine, in your best Morgan Freeman voice, God speaking these words to you: "Be still, and know that I am God." It can be said with such a tone as to humble us and bring us to our knees. Yet, the tone can also be a whisper of reassurance in your ear, reminding you of who is truly in control of each aspect of your life. It is a phrase of both fear and comfort.

Either way, God is telling you in this short verse to be still. He is putting your life on pause for a time to draw your attention to Him, to give to Him the control of your life that you currently think you have. In your situation, it may seem as if your world is falling apart—as if at the end of the day there is nothing or anyone left. Yet God is standing beside you, whispering into your ear, "Be still. I am God, and I have everything under control."

Notice the last line of the verse: "I will be exalted." Look around at the nations and the earth today. More people laugh in the face of God than would ever bow a knee in respect and reverence. Yet, in His thunderous voice, He guarantees that all people, all organizations, all governments, and all the world will kneel and exalt Him on a day that is coming.

In each area of your life, God is whispering, "Be still. I will be exalted in your trial!" And He's there to bring about good *in* you so that He may be exalted *by* you.

VALIANTLY WITH GOD

"With God we shall do valiantly;
it is he who will tread down our foes" ~Psalm 60:12

In this life you will meet many foes. Your foes might be sickness, loss of a job or relationship, or an actual foe—a real enemy, someone who is after your life and livelihood. It may be that someone doesn't like you, or someone may be jealous of you, or it may be because you are a Christ-follower. Whatever trial you presently find yourself in, your trial is also your foe. Just as a foe tries to destroy you or take you out of the fight, so does your trial.

The only One in existence who will *never* be your foe is Christ.

Only at the foot of the cross—in the power of Jesus Christ—can you overcome this trial courageously. Without God you will not come out of the valley stronger and full of life. It doesn't mean that the trial will continue or that your problems won't be solved—all trials at some point come to an end. Without Christ, though, there is no purpose in the trial; the trial is a waste. Without Christ you may walk out of the valley, but you will be no stronger than you were when you entered the valley. With Christ, you will walk out stronger, full of life—even if it means dying and going to heaven. Only Christ can defeat the enemies that sin has caused in our world of suffering.

God is fighting for you in every way to bring this trial to an end. The fight will end when He says it is over—and not a second before. He promises that He will strengthen you, and in His strength, you will be victorious—but only in His strength. In Him, and only in Him, you will do valiantly.

The only question is, will you let Him fight for you? Will you fight beside Him?

REMEMBER

"As for me, I would seek God, and to God would I commit my cause,
who does great things and unsearchable,
marvelous things without number" ~Job 5:8–9

If you haven not read through Job (or read through it recently), set aside some time to read through his story and experience his suffering. As you read, try to figure out how Job and his friends viewed God.

Early in his suffering, Job was met by three friends who would remain with him throughout the book. Job and his friends were unaware of the behind-the-scenes story between God and Satan—of God's allowing Satan to test and tempt Job. Satan's presence in Job's suffering did not diminish the responsibility of Job and his friends to have an accurate and appropriate view of the Lord. Even in his righteousness, Job didn't take the time (until the end of the book) to fully understand God and His role in suffering.

Finally, in chapter 37, God entered the scene to discuss His identity directly with Job. Job heard from God. The Lord made His appearance to show Job who He was (His character and His sovereignty), to humble Job's basic, small knowledge of Him, and to broaden Job's mind to the truth of God's existence and abilities.

Like Job, your suffering may be your opportunity, through the Bible, to have God reveal the true realities of Himself and His salvation to you. He will break you of false views and truly give you the truth of His grace and power to hold on to and dwell upon as you journey through the valley. Unlike Job, you have an opportunity to see and know that God is at work in your trial. You are aware that God is present; you have the advantage of having the Bible to know God. The Lord will work in your life beyond what you could imagine—in His ways, not yours. His presence, through the Spirit, should be encouragement and motivation to press on in the fight, dear Christ-follower.

I pray that you will long to know the Lord—not as you want to know Him, but as He wants to be known by you; not as you want Him to be, but just as He is. He is far greater than anything you could ever imagine or make up. Knowing who God is will make all the difference to understanding and overcoming your current situation. His Word is your window into His character and work for His saints.

Hold on to it, guard it, be grounded in it.

THE SCRIPTURES

"But rejoice insofar as you share Christ's sufferings, that you may also rejoice and be glad when his glory is revealed" ~1 Peter 4:13

Have you ever felt that the Bible was old and stale—as if it didn't apply to your sufferings or to our present world? One prayer I have for you is that you will see the Bible through new eyes while you are in your present struggle. I pray that you will read it with a new perspective, and that you will view God's Word as alive and vibrant in your life.

Martin Luther, a man who put his life on the line to start the Reformation in 1517, wrote: "Were it not for tribulation I should not understand the Scriptures." Trials and tribulations have a way of opening our eyes to the various depths of the Bible that we may have glossed over before.

You most likely desire to see God work in your suffering. The same God who wrote the Bible is the One who is going to work in your life. Whether He does big, mighty things or small, quiet things, He is still at work in your life.

My prayer for you is that in your trial you are clinging to your Bible. If you have not started a Bible reading plan before or during your trial, I highly encourage you to start—even one as simple as reading through the Psalms, which is a fantastic pursuit at any time of life. Reading scripture is going to ground you during this time. This is something we need at all times in life, but even more so during troubling times. There is great truth to be found in them, directing your thoughts toward Christ.

Your trial is hopefully giving you a new perspective on life and on the Word. During my own trial, I read the scriptures like I never had before, and I realized how present God was in the details of our lives. The Bible is God's Word—Him talking to us. In reading His Word, I knew these were God's words to His people. My pastor often says, "If you want to hear God speak, open His Word." God gave us His Word so that during times of suffering and times of joy, we can know God more, see His character, and become more like Christ. There was so much that I hadn't seen before, and every passage I read left me with a truth I could savor in my mind and dwell upon throughout whatever each day would bring. My eyes were opened even wider than they were previously, and I saw a greater goodness and presence of God than ever before. I pray that you will gain an understanding—a practical and real-life understanding—of what God is telling you in His Word. Yes, trials have a way of opening up the scriptures to us. God will certainly bless you in this pursuit, and it will give you great perspective on this life and on your relationship with the Lord.

God's working in the Bible and in your life serves two purposes: 1) to restore the relationship between Him and you, and 2) to bring Him glory. He is present in your trial, even if He seems quiet. At the right time He will act, according to His will, in your life. It is my prayer that you can rejoice, as Peter wrote in 1 Peter 4:13: "But rejoice insofar as you share Christ's suffering, that you may also rejoice and be glad when his glory is revealed."

A SAKE BEYOND YOUR OWN

*"Therefore I endure everything for the sake of the elect,
that they also may obtain the salvation that is in Christ Jesus
with eternal glory" ~2 Timothy 2:10*

One of the greatest things you can witness in this life is someone's salvation. As the church, the body of Christ, we rejoice in one person coming to Christ, and I can just imagine the rejoicing in heaven and on Christ's face when someone gives his or her life over to Him. Paul, in all of his tribulations, sees things as God does. He is willing to endure anything so that one person may be saved or so that one Christian may grow closer to Christ through Paul's own trial. Paul, in his plight, is planting seeds and planting churches wherever he goes and in every letter he writes. He's talking about the work of Christ throughout his own life and testimony so that others may be saved or exhorted in their life with Christ.

In your current struggles realize that God is using you and His story in you to plant seeds of faith for someone—or maybe for many people. The result may be that those seeds of faith will grow into salvation for someone.

In my trial of brain cancer, I had the great delight to see someone come to Christ in salvation through God's work in my life. Through my story, the Lord led one of His precious children to Him in faith. When I heard about this I realized that my cancer was worth it, and I would do it all over again if it meant that just one person would come to salvation. My prayer for you is that if one person is saved through your troubles or one Christian is encouraged in his or her faith, that you will find that it's all worth it. Just remember that God is using you far beyond what you could imagine or ever know in the lives of people you may never meet.

Will you say, as Paul did, "I endure everything for the sake of the elect"?

WHEN I FALL, I WILL RISE

*"Rejoice not over me, O my enemy; when I fall, I shall rise; when I sit in darkness,
the* Lord *will be a light to me" ~Micah 7:8*

We have all had someone dislike us, whether by our own doing or for
no reason of our own making. Of course, the tides are shifting in our
world, and someday there will be a great movement against those who
follow Christ. Persecution is coming—great or small. We have enemies,
and we should pray for them. Our enemies, in their sin, desire for us to
fall and to fail greatly. Micah tells us, though, that as Christ-followers we
will rise again because of the grace and power of God. It is God who
will vindicate and avenge us. (*Romans 12:14–21*)

In our trials we may feel like we have failed. When I was diagnosed
with brain cancer, I contemplated what I had been eating, how I might
have talked on my cell phone too much, or if I had grown up in a
polluted area. I felt, somehow, as if I had failed. Yet the doctors
reassured me that there was nothing within my control to have
prevented the cancer. I had no choice in this, and there was nothing I
could have done to stop it. For most of our trials, though not all, we
didn't and haven't failed. So rarely do we have control of our
circumstances.

You have no control over your enemies, just as you have no control
over your present struggles. From the gutters of life, where you probably
feel you are right now—that was how I felt—God will bend down from
the heights of heaven to lift you up for His glory.

One of the great gifts of our trials is the gift of perspective,
especially in the contrasts of the light and dark of this life. In our trials
we are in a valley, a place of darkness and despair. There is very little
light—if any at all—in valleys. You may feel like you are currently sitting
in darkness, and for some of you, it is the darkness of the hospital late at
night or in the early morning hours.

For a time, you will live each day in the darkness of suffering, yet my
prayer for you is that you will see all the more clearly the light of Christ.

He will be the light of life to you in the darkest of your days. In Christ, it does not matter how far you have fallen. You can trust that, in Christ, you will rise by His power.

.

WORTHY OF HIS CALLING

"To this end we always pray for you, that our God
may make you worthy of his calling and may fulfill every resolve for good and
every work of faith by his power, so that the name of our Lord Jesus may be glorified
in you, and you in him, according to the grace
of our God and the Lord Jesus Christ" ~2 Thessalonians 1:11–12

In many of his letters, Paul talks often about being worthy of the Lord's calling; it's one of his favorite phrases. God's call to salvation requires characteristics of righteousness that we do not innately possess, nor are we able to practice the righteousness God requires. He requires perfection, complete holiness, and righteousness without any questions. The only One who is able to meet these standards is Jesus, God's Son. Paul is saying that you cannot attain or become worthy of the Lord's calling on your own. He is saying that it is impossible without the power of Christ in your life. God called you, and it is He who will make you worthy of His calling. By the sacrifice of Christ, you will meet the requirements of the Lord.

Trials are one way that God makes you worthy of His calling. In a way, the trials of this life are the calling of the Lord upon you—that you may grow closer to Him and become more Christ-like. The calling of the Lord is a calling of you to Himself, a calling to throw aside the desires and trappings of this world and this life and to place in Him every hope, dream, and trust you may have.

Your trial is taking away the things you love in the world and bringing your focus onto Christ alone. His goal in this trial is that His kingdom will spread, that God will be glorified in you and through you, and that your relationship with Him will be strengthened. God promises that He is going to make you worthy of His calling, and in His call to worthiness, He is resolved to bring about His goodness for your sake and in His power.

Only in Christ can you live a life worth living.

LIVING BIBLE

"Only let your manner of life
be worthy of the gospel of Christ..." ~Philippians 1:27

You will meet many people on this journey of life. Your trial is an opportunity for people who have not yet followed Christ to see God at work in the very dire circumstances of your life. Most people these days have no idea of who God is, nor are they interested in what the Bible has to say about Him. Most people have discounted the Bible as ancient, old, dirty, and completely out of date in our modern and "superior" world. It has no use or purpose for them—or so they think. And yet, Jesus is exactly who this world needs, and we know that Jesus works through His Word and works in the lives of those who belong to Him.

While people may not believe in Him, they are sure to critique you and your faith based on your reaction to your circumstances. The spotlight is on *you* right now, Christ-follower. Believers and unbelievers alike are looking to you to show them the work of God in your life. They are wondering if Jesus is real and if your life will demonstrate whether He is real or false—all based on your response to your setbacks. As a Christ-follower you have the privilege of the presence of Christ. He is with you always. No matter your strength, weakness, or knowledge of Him, you are the one being watched for your thoughts and attitudes toward His work in your life. One purpose you have is to live out your faith—however difficult it presently is—to the glory of God. He is going to work in your life no matter what, and part of that work is Him working through you to show Himself to this unbelieving world. He desires that all people be saved, and He desires you to proclaim Him to everyone you meet. You will meet people while you are in the midst of your trial, and most of them will have no idea on the truth of Christ.

Your suffering is the Super Bowl of life; all eyes are upon you. As Pastor John MacArthur says, "You are the only Bible some unbelievers will ever read." Will you live in such a way that people will look at you and see Christ at work?

STEADFAST IN THE DEPTHS

Count it all joy, my brothers, when you meet trials of various kinds, for you know that the testing of your faith produces steadfastness. And let steadfastness have its full effect, that you may be perfect and complete, lacking nothing" ~James 1:2–4

In our trials and our circumstances, we wonder about our purpose and the reason we are undergoing such difficulties. James gives us the answer in verse 2: "The testing of your faith produces steadfastness." The Lord is looking for followers, His children, who will endure and persevere until the end. He is looking for those who will stay loyal in the good times and the bad times. He is not looking for fair-weather friends who are just in a relationship with Him for what they can get, yet, when the storm clouds billow, abandon Him, demonstrating the small faith they had.

Jesus loves us so much that He wants every part of us, and if we are honest with each other, we know that there are things in our lives that we are holding on to that detract from and weaken our relationship with Christ. James writes that our faith is being tested in order to move our hearts from this world toward the next, when we will be with Christ. The trials and tests of our lives on this earth are not in vain. They have purpose and meaning. James gives us one insight—among many in his book—to explain the purpose, which is to produce steadfastness.

In our lives we will face many trials, and if we are not facing a trial presently, we will at some point. Trials are a guarantee for the Christ-follower. Our trials may relate to our health, finances, relationships, or even to persecution for being a Christian. Persecution for Christ-followers is on the rise, both around the world and in the United States.

Christians can no longer live behind their community of faith but are confronted with their actual faith in Christ. Even if you are never persecuted for your faith, you will be persecuted for your morals, standards, and integrity, which for the Christian are all defined by Christ. James is showing us that when trials come—when persecution comes—we need to remain steadfast, to stay strong, to persevere in the storm.

We are called to live out our faith in our daily life until we are either called by the Lord into His presence or Jesus returns.

Your current journey is preparing you for a life of faith. Hold on to the Lord with each up and down, each new dawn and darkest night, in the calm breeze and raging winds, to go wherever He may take you.

Be steadfast and be strong in the Lord. It is He who will prevail over the darkness.

TORNADO

John Piper, pastor, speaker, and author, has such an elegant and humble way with his words and encouragement in spurring us on to a greater faith during these difficult times. He wrote an article titled, "Don't Waste Your Cancer," and while the overall topic is living in Christ with cancer, it truly should be titled, "Don't Waste Your Trial," for truly the wisdom therein will be a blessing to anyone going through difficult times. I hope you take time to read the article. (I listed the information below.)

One reason Piper writes this particular blog post is to clarify the reality of trials for the Christ-follower. He says, "God's design in the tornado of this cancer [your trial] is… 'to deepen my love for Christ…and to wean me off the breast of the world….' My tornado was a call to repentance." Piper echoes what Paul writes in Romans 12:2: "Be transformed" to the "will of God," to "goodness," and to perfection.

It is amazing that such a man of faith like Piper would say that this trial "was a call to repentance." It's easy to think that he, of all people, should be done repenting, and that he doesn't sin anymore. Yet the reality that Piper brings to us is that one of God's intentions in our trial is to tear our hearts from the world and to anchor our souls in Him. Piper realizes that each of us sins every day; some of us sin more, and some sin less, but sin is a part of all of our lives, and we need to continue to seek the Lord in repentance. We will not reach perfection until we die. Even the strongest Christ-follower you know still struggles with sin in this life. Piper doesn't want to waste his trial by not realizing that he can grow closer to Christ at any stage of life. Any trial, whether caused by sin or not, is God's personal call to you to grow closer to Him, to abide in His presence, "to be transformed."

An amazing resource for you is Piper's sermon titled, "Christ and Cancer." While he may talk about cancer as an example, the blessing comes in Christ during this very dark journey you are on—whatever suffering you are presently facing.

The goal of God in every part of our lives is for Him to change us into the likeness of His Son, Jesus Christ. Are you willing to allow the tornadoes you are going through to bring you closer to the Lord?

* * *

http://www.desiringgod.org/blog/posts/clarifying-the-tornado

http://www.desiringgod.org/sermons/christ-and-cancer

BLESSED ARE...

"And he opened his mouth and taught them saying: 'Blessed are the poor in spirit, for theirs is the kingdom of heaven. Blessed are those who mourn, for they shall be comforted. Blessed are the meek, for they shall inherit the earth. Blessed are those who hunger and thirst for righteousness, for they shall be satisfied. Blessed are the merciful, for they shall receive mercy. Blessed are the pure in heart, for they shall see God. Blessed are the peacemakers, for they shall be called sons of God. Blessed are those who are persecuted for righteousness' sake, for theirs is in the kingdom of heaven. Blessed are you when others revile you and persecute you and utter all kinds of evil against you falsely on my account. Rejoice and be glad, for your reward is great in heaven, for so they persecuted the prophets who were before you'" ~Matthew 5:2–12

As you read the passage above, were you able to identify with any of the groups Jesus talks about?

Time after time in this passage Jesus talks about different groups of people and the promises He makes to them. He talks about the poor in spirit, those who mourn, the meek, those who hunger and thirst, the innocent, those who try to make peace, the persecuted, and the reviled. Each group is distinct, relating to a particular type of person or situation, and yet you may find similarity between these groups and your present circumstances.

In the tough times of life, God has reserved a special blessing for you. God's calling for you has its sacrifices, but it also has its rewards, the greatest of which is Christ Himself. God is going to reward you and leave you with peace as you walk through this dark valley. He is present with you. He is the blessing. The rewards may come in this life, but the ultimate—and greater—reward is yet to come in heaven, where you will be in the physical presence of Christ.

It is time to prepare for the time when you will stand in His presence.

THE GATE OF THE FEW

"Enter by the narrow gate. For the gate is wide and the way is easy that leads to destruction, and those who enter by it are many.
For the gate is narrow and the way is hard that leads to life, and those who find it are few" ~Matthew 7:13–14

Doesn't it seem that for some people life is so easy? They have the perfect family, perfect job, perfect neighborhood, and they're friends with everyone. Or maybe I am just thinking of everyone on social media. Anyway, God's calling on our lives as Christians is not to a life of rest and relaxation in this world—though we may have periods of time where we can do that. God's calling is much grander than sitting on the beaches of Hawaii. Many of us are pursuing the same things as everyone else—a nice life with the comforts of living in America or other Western cultures. Our lives tend to look no different than anyone else's. It's not a bad thing to pursue and provide the best for your family. However, where we err in this perspective and the pursuits of our hearts is that we think that this is all that God wants for our lives on this earth.

God's calling for our lives in this world is very different. He's calling us to live lives that are drastically different from the rest of the world: to pursue Christ over pretending to be perfect people, to pursue Christ over material things, to pursue Christ over an easy, comfortable life. Our lives in Christ are just that: intended to pursue Christ. The church is just as handicapped by materialism as the world. The reality is that so many who are handcuffed to this world will not reach the life beyond. Sadly, this is the case for the majority. But God's desire is to bring all to salvation, that all would accept Him as their Lord and Savior.

However, those who choose the path Christ set forth for you will have life, but the road to that life is very hard. Life is going to have its troubles and difficulties, and if you are in one right now, think beyond the present struggle to what's coming later. By choosing the narrow path—and thus, the narrow gate—by choosing Christ, real life awaits you. It is a call to live differently in every way, to make every decision with Christ in mind, to build every relationship with Christ at the center, and to live with the desire to glorify Christ in every area of your life. It's hard, but the reward is great—eternal life in Christ, which is far greater than having the perfect life, or pretending to have the perfect life.

There aren't many who willingly and gladly lay down their desires and their very lives at the feet of Christ and allow Him to work through and in them for His glory and ultimate salvation, as well as for the salvation of those who are watching them. Few find Christ in their trials. Few find joy in this God-ordained path. I am praying that you will be one of the few!

In your trial, you are on the narrow road, but you must decide whether to stay on this road. The wide road is always easier, always more popular. Which road are you going to choose? The choice is yours.

ORDAINED TO HAPPEN

"Who has spoken and it came to pass,
unless the Lord has commanded it? Is it not from the mouth of the Most High that
good and bad come?" ~Lamentations 3:37–38

There are two amazing truths in this passage from the prophet Jeremiah:
1) the Lord has allowed your trial, and 2) the Lord works all things for
His glory in the good and the bad you face in this life. It is similar to the
story of Job.

First, there is nothing that happens in this life without His allowing
it to happen. In His wisdom and with His reasoning the Lord has
ordained this trial in your life. He has allowed this trial for a specific
purpose in your life—primarily for His glory—to bring you closer to
Him.

Second, Jeremiah writes that God allows both good and bad in our
lives. He allows the easy times and the hard times, both of which are to
bring Him glory. Most likely we will not understand His will in allowing
good and bad in our lives. We won't see the entire picture of His
sovereign hand while on this side of heaven. We need to rest in the fact
that all is within His power and control. The purpose is for His glory,
remember though, He has purpose in it for you personally, as well as a
purpose in it for others.

Mankind's sin has brought the bad things into this world. God does
not cause us to sin; we can do that well enough on our own. However,
at no point in our sinful world did God lose control of this world. It is
always His, and He can turn the bad things of our lives around for good.

LET THE WAVES PASS

"Fear not, for I am with you; be not dismayed, for I am your God;
I will strengthen you, I will help you,
I will uphold you with my righteous right hand" ~Isaiah 41:10

My pastor, Todd Smith, was one of a small band of brothers and sisters who from the beginning of my journey with cancer walked every minute and beyond with me. Each gave encouragement and exhortation in my walk with Christ, and each was a human presence that made the darkness of my trials so much easier. They were a committed and—dare I say it? —a motley crew.

A week after my first brain surgery, when things were looking very grim in terms of treatment options and long-term prognosis, my pastor sent me this text message: "Continue to let the waves of fear crash over you and meet God on the other side." He knew exactly what I was encountering, and he knew the exact words I needed to hear.

I was facing a huge wave, just as you might be facing one as you read this. You may have a meeting that you don't want to have, a doctor's appointment that may confirm your greatest fear, a conversation with a friend that may not turn out so well. The wave is coming. It will envelope you. It will hurt and be unpleasant. But welcome it and let it crash over you; God is on the other side, waiting for you. When you go through the wave, you can rest in the fact, that in order for Him to meet you on the other side, it had to go over Him first. Though the waves crash, the Lord will "uphold you with [His] righteous right hand." He knows the difficulty you face; He has faced it Himself. And like all the trials of our world, this too shall pass. The seas will calm down; the sun will shine again; the storm will end; and the salty air will flow onto your face, bringing peace, contentment, and joy.

My prayer is that you will lay the battles you face at the foot of the cross, for "[He] will strengthen you, [He] will help you."

THE MOST INCREDIBLE JOURNEY

"If you then, who are evil, know how to give good gifts to your children, how much
more will your Father who is in heaven
give good things to those who ask him!" ~Matthew 7:11

Can we consider our trials a gift from God? Can we honestly and
faithfully do that? Can you stand in the storm, rain pelting, wind
shrieking, waves breaking and crashing, and truly praise the Lord? At the
end of the day, after you have endured weeks, months, maybe years of
pain and heartache, wondering when it would all end, can you stand
before the Lord and say "Thank you?"

This may sound strange, but I have come to look at my cancer as a
great gift from God. It wasn't easy, and my life will never—and *can*
never—be the same again. But I look at the amazing things the Lord did
through those oppressive and difficult months, and I cannot help but
praise the Lord for all that He did and all the things I couldn't and
wouldn't have learned any other way. It was the most incredible journey
with my Savior. The things I learned could only be learned through the
storms of life. The relationships that blossomed with God and others
may not have been as deep without the cancer. I saw the church and my
fellow brothers and sisters in Christ come alive. They grew in prayer, in
reading the Bible, and in encouraging one another. They were growing
in Christ, just as I was growing in Christ.

The best thing was that God was there with me each step of the
way, and He and I grew very close, because when there wasn't
someone's hand to hold, His Word was always there to read or to
meditate on. I truly felt the Lord's presence—in the spirit—every step of
every day.

There were days full of doubt and questioning of the Lord—you
and I are only human!—but God proved Himself faithful beyond my
expectations. This trial is far from over and will, most likely, be a
shadow in my life until I go to be with the Lord, but I am better for it.

The challenges I faced grew me as a man and most of all as a Christ-follower.

In the end, my prayer for you is that you will look back on your trial as a great gift from God. It may not be today, tomorrow, or a year from now. I just pray that you will look back on this valley and see what God has done and has accomplished in you—and also in many others—through your journey. You are constantly in my prayers.

If evil people give good gifts, think how great the gifts of the Lord are. And truly our trials are gifts.

THE FALLOW FIELD

"For we are God's fellow workers.
You are God's field, God's building" ~1 Corinthians 3:9

Have you ever wandered by a field that's been left fallow—or as we say in the city, the vacant lot? It's abandoned; weeds grow everywhere. The plants grow wild, animals and spiders may have made their homes and nests there. The reality is that it's been left alone by itself for far too long. The field is capable of growing great crops, plants, and fruits, but it's just sitting there, not living up to its potential.

The reality is that for this field to bear fruit, to be more than it currently is, it has to be plowed. It cannot be left alone in idleness. The plowshare must break the hardened, stubborn soil, and the field's comfortable and apathetic life must be challenged. As the plowshare digs deep lines into the difficult soil, the land struggles to allow the plowshare to do its work. It fights back, unyielding and inflexible, like many of us are. However, as the soil gets cut and scarred, the land opens up, allowing the planter to irrigate it, to plant seeds, and to eventually see growth, and the fruit of his or her labor. The field becomes more productive and fruitful as a result of the work of a farmer versus being left alone by itself.

As you allow the Lord to work in your life—through the pain and difficulty of any trial—you are allowing Him to dig deep into the soil of your soul and plant the seed of His Word deep into your life. Hosea, the Old Testament prophet, rightly alludes to God's work in our lives when he writes, "Sow for yourselves righteousness; reap steadfast love, break up your fallow ground, for it is the time to seek the LORD, that he may come and rain righteousness upon you." (*Hosea 10:12*)

It's not easy being plowed over, but the fruits that come from it in the end are worth it, and others will be blessed through your struggle.

The Lord is working in your life, not always by your choosing, but by His. Remember this: as a Christ-follower, you are His, and He will work in your life as He desires and wills. As the potter works with the clay, so does God work in the field: "You are God's field, God's building."

God does not build facades that might crumble at the slightest wind. He builds buildings that weather the storm and are stronger because of it. This plowing over is hard—as you are most likely experiencing—but the growth and fruit is greater than the pain.

And His fields always yield fruit.

HOPE, PATIENCE, PRAYER

"Rejoice in hope, be patient in tribulation,
be constant in prayer" ~Romans 12:12

In this passage from Romans, Paul is describing the life of those who
are truly devoted to Christ. He gets to this part in Romans 12, which
should be an anthem cry for anyone in the midst of a trial, or dare I say,
the entire life of the Christ-follower: "Rejoice in hope, be patient in
tribulation, be constant in prayer." Paul writes three parts in one
beautiful anthem.

Rejoice in hope. Part of God's purpose in our trials is to strip from
our sight the things of this world. God is showing you that, compared to
Him, the world cannot hold your gaze, focus, or attention. God wants to
take the things you are holding on to in this world so that you will
redirect your sight upon Him. He holds your hope. You can rest and
rejoice in what He has done, in what He will do, in His continual
presence, and work in your life.

Be patient in tribulation. Waiting is a natural part of life, but in
trials it seems to be a *large* part of life. Waiting for that call for the job
interview, waiting for the test results, waiting in the doctor's office,
waiting for your loved one to come home—it seems that sometimes
there is endless waiting. The truth is that in our trials we are already on
edge and impatient. We like to say that we are patient, but the reality is
that so very few of us have this incredible gift of patience. Yet God is
asking us to wait, and this is an opportunity to practice patience.

Remember that things happen in the Lord's timing, not ours. How
the Lord works is one of the greatest mysteries we may never figure out
this side of heaven, and even *then*, we may never know. Peter writes,
"With the Lord one day is as a thousand years, and a thousand years as
one day." (*2 Peter 3:8*)

God doesn't work within our time frames or in the constraints of a
twenty-four-hour day. He is outside the confines of this world and will

work within time only as He sees fit. He has absolutely perfect timing: He is never early, and He is never late. And He will work in and through your trial as He wills.

Be constant in prayer. "Pray without ceasing" (*1 Thessalonians 5:17*), is written as a command to constantly pray, no matter the circumstance. The goal is to always be in communication with the Lord. Since His Spirit is always with you as a Christ-follower, He is more than eager to listen to your heartfelt praises, prayers, and pleas during the good and bad of your life. Prayer is an incredible action—probably the one thing you do as a Christ-follower that the Lord loves more than any other. It is His way of hearing your heart—not in flattery, but in reality. He longs to hear your heart and your thoughts. He longs for you to be absolutely vulnerable and transparent with Him and yet to also trust and rely in the promises put forth in His Word. In your exhaustion, pray. Just talk to the Lord, and amazingly, He will renew your strength and spirit. He loves to hear your voice speak truth and dependence on Him.

The challenge in any part of life is to consistently rejoice, be patient, and pray. You have been given such an opportunity, as hard as it is, to practice these spiritual skills. Remember, He is right beside you, waiting to hear your voice.

A PRAYER TO THE END

*"To this end we always pray for you, that our God may make you worthy of his
calling and may fulfill every resolve for good and every work of faith
by his power, so that the name of our Lord Jesus may be glorified in you, and you in
him, according to the grace of our God
and the Lord Jesus Christ" ~2 Thessalonians 1:11–12*

My hope for you is that you have people who are committed to the Lord
interceding on your behalf to Him. Even if you think no one is praying
for you, know that I am. I do not know your name or your
circumstances, but I am praying for your relationship with the Lord, that
He will work out His will in your life, that you will grow closer to Him,
and become more like Him during this trial. He is going to act in His
time, according to His will, for the sake of your soul to make you worthy
of the calling He has already placed upon you as a Christ-follower. He is
seeking to be glorified in your life. Though life may seem dark right
now, He wants to shine His light in you and through you so that you
may be a faithful witness to His character and salvation.

The church, under Christ, is called to always pray. Sometimes the
church, as a whole, fails in lifting up its members to the Lord. Your trial
is an opportunity for Christ to display Himself. In the church is a small,
incredible group of people called to pray, no matter the need. I hope
that in your suffering you will seek out these people. I desire for them to
entreat the Lord on your behalf. It truly brings them great joy to do
this—even for those who do not know you.

As you seek Christ in your trial, I pray that you will also seek those
who will pray for you and minister to you.

NOT JUST YOURS

"Now when Job's three friends heard of all this evil that had come upon him, they came each from his own place....
They made an appointment together to come to show him sympathy and comfort him.... And they sat with him on the ground seven days and seven nights, and no one spoke a word to him, for they saw that his suffering was very great" ~Job 2:11–13

This may not be what you want to hear, but this journey you are on is not just yours. Yes, you are the one who has to go through it—whether it's pain, loss, or desperation. But the reality is that someone is walking with you or observing you through this journey. There are people—most likely family and friends—who will be physically present with you either throughout the entire journey, or just a part of the journey. Undoubtedly, there will also be people who are watching you and your walk with Christ during your storm. Some are watching to see if your faith in Christ is real, and some are watching to see the genuineness of your faith. You may know some of those who will watch from afar, but more than likely, you will never know everyone who is watching.

The day I was diagnosed with cancer I learned whose journey this would also be. It was mine of course. No one else could undergo my tests, surgeries, chemo, radiation, or all of the side effects of those treatments. But there was a significant group of people who, from that very first day, wanted to learn and grow closer to Christ, just as I was doing, and they were willing to walk each step of the journey with me. They couldn't take away the pain; they couldn't lie in the hospital bed for me. But they were as much a part of this journey in God's eyes as I was, and each committed himself or herself to growing in Christ, just as I desired to do.

I learned something very early on: my cancer may not have been about me at all. Like Job, I don't get to see the totality of my trial; I saw only a small part—just as you see only a small part of your journey. I may not get to see all the people encouraged or challenged through the trial or even the people who came to Christ because of my trial, but I, like you, will see some purpose—maybe not today or tomorrow, but one day. Some were there for parts of the storm, while others endured the entirety of it. It was their choice as to how much of the journey they would walk with me or even if they wanted to walk this journey at all.

Look at Job's trial and the friends who sat with him for days on end. Job did not choose who came to sit with him, but they each grew because of his trial, learned just as Job did, and grew closer to the Lord by the end of the book. Hopefully your friends are better (and wiser) than Job's; nevertheless, your journey has lessons for everyone.

The reality is that as great as your friends and family are, there is only One who will entirely walk this journey with you—Jesus Christ. He has set His Spirit upon you as a Christ-follower. The psalmist writes in Psalm 94:14: "For the LORD will not forsake his people; he will not abandon his heritage." What an astonishing thought that, in Christ, He makes us a part of His heritage.

REFUGE

*"He who dwells in the shelter of the Most High will abide
in the shadow of the Almighty. I will say to the LORD,
'My refuge and my fortress, my God, in whom I trust.'
For he will deliver you from the snare of the fowler and from the deadly pestilence. He
will cover you with his pinions, and under his wings you will find refuge; His
faithfulness is a shield and buckler" ~Psalm 91:1–4*

People are sick and dying; relationships and families are broken; governments and leaders are corrupt and failing; persecution of Christians is growing (even in America); and countries are at war. On a good day you can see that the world is crumbling all around you and crying out for someone to save it. You're in this world and currently suffering. You may not know where to turn, who to turn to, or what the next step of your journey will be. Has God become "your refuge and your fortress"? Have you found security in Christ? His fortress is one that is sure and steady; it will never crumble or fall. Are you finding your refuge in Him?

There is only One who can come to your aid and your help during this time—Jesus Christ, Him alone. I hope you have friends and family with you on this journey, though always remember that Christ was with you from before the beginning of time and on into eternity, which has no end—ever. He knew the way into the trial, and only He knows the way through the trial to the end, because Christ has walked a similar journey. He is your refuge and your strength through this, and only He can provide everything you need to persevere.

I pray that there are people who will lift you up in prayer to Christ. If no one is with you, trust in the fact that God is there. He's with you from the beginning and will remain until the end of this journey. Also, please know that I pray for you every day. Though I may not know your name or story, as Christians, we are called to walk this life together. So let me tell you again that I walk this road with you in prayer. In verse 4 the psalmist writes that God's "faithfulness is a shield and buckler." Christ is not going to leave you alone during this time of adversity. The fiery darts of this life—your trials—must go through Him first to get to you. He knows each pierce, each burn, each blow, and each cut, and in keeping His promises, He chooses to stay with you. There is nowhere you can go, no action you can take, that Christ has not already seen or walked in before. At times He may be silent, but He is present with you in every way. It is a truth that He will never leave you, and you must hold on to that promise as you endure.

Make Him your shield! And rest in the fact that God is mightily working in your life, even in areas you cannot see.

DON'T LOSE HEART

"So we do not lose heart. Though our outer self is wasting away, our inner self is being renewed day by day. For this slight momentary affliction is preparing for us an eternal weight of glory beyond all comparison, as we look not to the things that are seen but to the things that are unseen. For the things that are seen are transient, but the things that are unseen are eternal" ~2 Corinthians 4:16–18

The reality for all of us is this: we are getting older, and our bodies are deteriorating. Yes, I know it's not nice to call someone old, but let's face it, we are either old now, or we will be someday. We can literally see our outer nature wasting away, and no chemicals or surgery can change that—unless we want to look plastic or robotic.

Christ-follower, you are not simply growing older, but you are growing better. Your body will fail at some point, you will physically die, but your spirit and soul will live on into eternity. Some of the youngest, most youth-filled, energized, and joyful people on this earth are the senior Christ-followers in our churches and at the senior centers. Our time on this earth is temporary, and our physical bodies are quickly fading. Each day we live is one day closer to our eternal purpose in Christ.

Notice that Paul says, "this slight momentary affliction." Paul faced physical trial after physical trial for most of his Christian life. How could he call everything he went through a momentary affliction? Compared with eternity your affliction is momentary. It is passing, and something greater is coming—an eternal life with Christ. Paul couldn't even put into words the joys of the next life. He could only say that it is "beyond comparison." The reality for Paul was that there was nothing he knew—and nothing we know—that could compare to what is coming in eternity. In the next life, the "weight of glory" he speaks of, is not at all a negative weight, but it is the fact that we will be present with Christ and be like Christ. We will see Christ as He is. Looking to Christ, Paul could say with all his strength that the trials of this life were slight and momentary. As hard as it is to believe right now, your trial will be slight and momentary also. The weight of your sin and the problems of the world will no longer be upon your shoulders. As Christ says, "My yoke is easy, and my burden is light." *(Matthew 11:30)*

In Christ, the weight of our present lives and struggles will be changed into a life in which we will be present before the Lord—for all eternity.

PONDERING WEIGHTY THINGS

"Therefore, since we are surrounded by so great a cloud of witnesses, let us also lay aside every weight, and sin which clings so closely, and let us run with endurance the race that is set before us, looking to Jesus, the founder and perfecter of our faith, who for the joy set before him endured the cross, despising the shame, and is seated at the right hand of the throne of God" ~Hebrews 12:1–2

There is no better place for pondering the weighty things of life than in a hospital room. You are hooked up to all of these machines; you cannot move, sleep, or get comfortable; it is dark and noisy; and the rest you need is broken by just being in the hospital. Hospitals are no place for rest, but they are a place to ponder the heavy things in life, your walk with God, what comes next in life, your relationships, and your place and purpose in this world. And while you're lying there, hearing the machines beep in the background, the world continues on, living "normal" lives with little regard to the many who are suffering. Of course, for many of us, another place we ponder weighty things is late into the night, while we lie in our beds, staring at the ceiling.

John Piper writes in *Future Grace*, "God was keeping me back from excessive vanity and worldliness. He was causing me to ponder weighty things in solitude, while many others were breezily slipping into superficial patterns of life." God wants you to grow in your relationship with Him, to become more like Christ. In His sovereignty, God Almighty chose to take some comforts of this world away from you so that He could work in your life. Think about it this way: God chose this time for you to be close to Him. You get to see Him directly working in your life, whether in large ways or in the small things.

You have been given an incredible gift in the form of your trial. Like Piper says, others were living superficial lives. The Lord is forcing you to take your eyes and focus off this world and turn them toward greater things—the Lord Himself. Isn't that so much better than who wins the game, your car, what you look like, how many kids you have, where you live, the size of your home, how green your grass is, or the amount in your bank account? The list could go on and on of things that can distract you from your relationship with Him. Your walk with Christ should be of utmost importance in your life, but so often Christ is just an add-on, a second thought to our materialistic, boastful, false lives.

We live in a world of shallow people, and sadly, many of our churches are filled with shallow and nominal Christians. Just take a look at any social media platform. We like to pretend life is a certain way to make others think good things about us. It is like living on the beach when God is calling us out to deeper waters to experience His grace. Yet we are content living life just like everyone else. We just add Christ to the lives we have built to impress our Christian friends.

Are we Christ-followers, or are we the Joneses? So many Christians look no different from anyone else, except that they may go to church—and even then, probably not faithfully. Trials are God-given opportunities to live like Christ, to take our eyes off this world, and to focus completely and absolutely on Him alone. This is much better than looking for the greener grass on the other side.

Ponder the weighty things of life and be better for it, because God is in the weighty things of this life. God gives us a great gift in our suffering—Himself.

NO PLAGUE

"Because you have made the LORD your dwelling place—the Most High, who is my refuge—no evil shall be allowed to befall you, no plague come near your tent. For he will command his angels concerning you to guard you in all your ways. On their hands they will bear you up, lest you strike your foot against a stone. You will tread on the lion and the adder; the young lion and the serpent you will trample underfoot" ~Psalm 91:9–13

God has demonstrated in Psalm 91 the protection for those who wholeheartedly follow Him and belong to Him. That does not mean that your faith will not waver, but it does mean that God's presence in your life would not waver—not one bit. God's promises in verses 9–13 are quite remarkable. The psalmist writes: "No evil shall be allowed to befall you," and even more strongly, "No plague come near your tent." I know you may be thinking that a plague came near your tent, especially if you are dealing with sickness. A plague is a bad thing: it kills; it spreads; and it's relentless. God has a relentless promise that your trial is not a plague, but it is isolated in scope and purpose. You will not be utterly destroyed in this present suffering. Yes, life will change, and it may change dramatically. Know and trust that all is within His scope and His purpose.

One of our limitations as people is that we are unaware of the spiritual warfare happening around us. There is no doubt that spiritual warfare is happening around you. As Job was unaware of what was happening behind the scenes of his own suffering, so we, in our own lives, are unaware of the totality of God's working and of what He may be allowing.

However, we are not left unprotected. God is present with us, and in the warfare of your trial, angels are fighting alongside Him for your protection and your good. He will "guard you in all your ways." Even the spiritual warfare that may be occurring around you is under His control. With God and His angels beside you there is nothing you need to fear, and I hope you feel like you can do anything (within the limits of His will, of course). God has conquered the world, and with God by your side you share in His triumph. You will walk valiantly through this trial because the Lord will be right beside you each step of the way. Even if that means dying, you will walk triumphantly to heaven.

HE'S ALREADY THERE

"Come now, you who say, 'Today or tomorrow we will go into such and such a town and spend a year there and trade and make a profit'—yet you do not know what tomorrow will bring. What is your life? For you are a mist that appears for a little time and then vanishes" ~James 4:13–14

Tomorrow is always a daring prospect. Sometimes we face tomorrow with delight, sometimes with great anxiety. We pretend we know what tomorrow will bring, but we are unprepared for any unexpected bumps in the road. The reality for all of us is that we do not really know what tomorrow will bring. We may know bits and pieces of what may happen tomorrow, but we never truly know until we get there. There is only One who knows; it is the Lord.

When I had my two brain surgeries in the summer of 2014, I was always a bit anxious the day before. I think anyone would be. Yet my pastor reminded me of something: God was already there in tomorrow's surgeries. He knew the outcome, and He knew the prognosis.

God does not worry, because God is not constrained by time, and He knows all the answers and outcomes to everything. He knows your past, your present, and your tomorrow—all at the same time. In knowing this, I am not afraid of tomorrow, because I know God is already there, and He is there in your tomorrow, waiting for you. God is presently with you, and He is preparing your tomorrow for you.

You may be facing a diagnosis, a job interview, a court date, a meeting with someone who hurt you, upcoming bills, or surgery tomorrow or a week away. You worry about what's going to happen and wonder about the outcome of whatever you're facing. Take courage. As a Christ-follower, you serve a God who is presently with you and is also waiting for you in your tomorrow. He knows your entire story: the beginning, middle, and the end. He has never failed you, and He never will.

Think about this: God has already finished writing history. The book of Revelation, as confusing as it can be, is the end of history. God knows the end of history, because He is already there, just as He is already in your tomorrow. He knows the entirety of your story while you live it out here on earth.

Take heart in what Moses spoke to the people of Israel in Deuteronomy 31:6: "Be strong and courageous. Do not fear or be in dread of them, for the LORD your God who goes with you, He will not leave you or forsake you."

PRUNED BY THE MASTER

"Every branch in me that does not bear fruit he prunes
that it may bear more fruit" ~John 15:2

On the side of my childhood home we had a small area for rose bushes. Several times a year my dad would prune them or cut them back. I never understood why he did this. He was taking away what seemed to be healthy parts of the plant, thereby shrinking the size of the rose bushes. Dad explained to me that pruning actually made the roses healthier, bursting with more blooms, and producing a stronger, more bountiful harvest.

It is the same with vineyards. The vinedresser, or caretaker of the vineyard, does the same thing in order to bring about a larger harvest, a tastier fruit.

This passage in John 15:1–17 is one of the last teachings of Jesus. He is talking to His disciples at His last meal, which we call the Last Supper. Always one who is great with His words, He says that God's relationship with us is like that of a vinedresser to his vines. There are many metaphors in this passage, but the best one to hear in our suffering is that there is purpose. Truly, we serve a God who has many purposes within each minute of our lives.

Pruning roses and vines is never easy, and it is not without its pain. For us, trials are the pruning in our lives. They are part of our sanctification in Christ. He is a careful vinedresser though, carefully pruning individual aspects of our lives. We hurt, we cry, we think it will never end. He is not haphazard about it, as some may be, slashing and hacking. No, He knows each part of our lives that He is working on, bringing about greater fruit for His kingdom.

There are many purposes in pruning, and one way God prunes us is through the trials and the sufferings of this life. He could have left you the way you were, and if you think about it, you may want Him to, but He wants you to grow—to produce more fruit for His kingdom. A vine or rose bush may grow large without pruning, it may produce fruit, but it is weak fruit, poor fruit. It is not a fruit that people want, nor is it attractive. But God didn't leave you alone. He chose you; He loves you; and He knows that pruning is the best thing for you. Under the hand, direction, and careful pruning of God you become a better person.

I pray that you will find it a joy to have the Father prune your life—as hard as it may seem. Are you willing to have the Lord work in you to create a better, more Christ-centered life?

HELP FROM THE LORD

"I lift up my eyes to the hills. From where does my help come? My help comes from the LORD, who made heaven and earth. He will not let your foot be moved; he who keeps you will not slumber. Behold, he who keeps Israel will neither slumber nor sleep. The LORD is your keeper; The LORD is your shade on your right hand. The sun shall not strike you by day, nor the moon by night. The LORD will keep you from all evil; he will keep your life. The LORD will keep your going out and your coming in from this time forth and forevermore" ~Psalm 121

When trouble arrives, where does your help come from? Where do you get advice and guidance? Is there anyone who can give you wisdom to help you navigate the maze of your life on this journey? We can find "answers" in this world, but those will still leave us wondering and questioning. We may get answers from doctors, employment seminars, counseling, or self-help books, but do they really answer the ultimate question: "Who is in control of all this?" It is a question that, no matter our beliefs or ideology, we all ask. Even if we deny it, we still wonder.

So much of our world and our lives are outside of our control that it makes us think that someone or something is entirely in charge. We may believe we are here by chance or that our lives are made up of random occurrences and experiences. But deep, deep within us is this hope that there is someone in control.

It brings us back to the question in verse 1: "From where does my help come?" The psalmist answers it immediately, giving no time to look to the help of this world, and says, "My help comes from the Lord, who made heaven and earth." There is no doubt in the author's mind that it is the Lord—and the Lord alone—who has everything within His grasp and control. There is no other person, being, idea, or theory that creates and controls the world. It is the Lord alone.

The writer then goes on to describe the Lord and His many splendored attributes, emphasizing that wherever we are in life, in the ups and downs, we may find great encouragement here. He says that the Lord is not moved by anyone or anything but Himself. He does not sleep, because He doesn't need rest. There is nothing powerful enough to exhaust Him. Where you and I need constant rest and sleep, He doesn't need either. As Christ-followers, we can be assured that He is our keeper, walking with us through each heartbeat of our lives. There is nothing that can hurt us without Him allowing it for His greater purpose and glory. He is the one who will keep our life and preserve it, until the day He calls us home—not a day too soon or a day too late. He is personally involved in every movement and step we take. He is the preserver of life—each breath and each heartbeat.

The psalmist ends by describing the length of time the Lord will be involved in your life: "from this time forth and forevermore." From the beginning of your days until the end of eternity, Jesus is managing your entire life. That is a truth you can hold on to in your suffering. You play a part in His story, in redeeming His people, in giving Him the glory in your life, "from this time forth and forevermore."

Are you looking to the Lord to answer all of your questions and doubts? Are you allowing Him to guide you through the storm?

SHAME THE STRONG

"But God chose what is foolish in the world to shame the wise; God chose what is weak in the world to shame the strong" ~1 Corinthians 1:27

God is always working against the world system that we know and live in, and the truth is, God does not work on our terms, but on His, and His terms are always unexpected. You and your trial have a role in the way God is working in our world.

No one likes to be called foolish or weak, and I do not want to call you either one here. What I do want to call you, and I think God does too, is unexpected. Think about how God works. He is choosing those the world would never choose, so that through them He can do His mighty works. The world expects history to be made by the wise and the strong. It is natural for us to expect the wise and the strong to be in control of the world, and yet God chooses to work against the world to accomplish His purpose in the lives of people.

Think about David—an unexpected choice to be king of Israel. Think about the disciples from the backwaters of Galilee, especially Peter. As a group, they were people unexpected to be closest to Jesus, chosen to work with Jesus for three years, to build Christ's church all around the world. Think about Esther and how God used her to save the Jewish people. Or think about Moses, for that matter, leading the Jews to the Promised Land. Lastly, think about Jesus. Yes, He is God, but consider where His earthly family was from— "nowhere Nazareth." From the middle of nowhere came the Savior of the world. Completely unexpected. These people were never expected to amount to much (except Jesus), and God did not choose them because of their capability or incapability. So why did He choose them? Why did He choose you?

Would you be offended if I said that He chose you not because of you, but because of Him? Regardless, He did. He chose your trial uniquely for you because of the work He can do in and through your circumstances. All He asks from you is a willingness to follow Him wherever He desires. God is going to work in your life whether you want Him to or not. Willingly walking with Him down the paths of His choosing, though, is one of the most astounding journeys you could ever take in this life. It's not logical at all, but God doesn't always work according to human logic.

Remember, whenever you feel weak or that you don't fit in anywhere, you can trust that God has great plans to use you in His kingdom and for His glory. You are the unexpected person that God is going to use to change a person's life, or to possibly change the world.

THE JOY BEFORE YOU

"Looking to Jesus, the founder and perfecter of our faith, who for the joy that was set before him endured the cross, despising the shame, and is seated at the right hand of the throne of God" ~Hebrews 12:2

One of the amazing things about a simple Bible verse is that just a few words contains a mountain of wisdom. Jesus knows the pain and hurt you're going through; the only difference is that He endured a greater degree than you. His sufferings and pains were immense while He was on this earth, including His excruciating execution on the cross. His physical, emotional, and spiritual pain far outweigh any pain a simple human could ever endure. He knows how to suffer, and He knows each pain and heartache that you are currently enduring, because He too had great pain and heartache. He is intimately involved in your life—always has been, and always will be. It is hard to look at His life and your current life on this journey as a happy and joyous one.

Think about the statement: "For the joy that was set before Him endured the cross." Why would Jesus, who was enduring the worst death possible, physically, emotionally, and spiritually consider it a joy? Why would He embrace it with this attitude and mind-set?

Think about it this way. Physically, Christ was scourged, beaten; His back and head were torn open by whips and thorns; His hands and feet were nailed to a piece of wood. Emotionally, the religious elite and the people of Israel betrayed Him. Even His own disciples, His friends and family, turned on Him. Spiritually, He bore the greatest anguish. He carried the weight of our sin and guilt. Even greater was the fact that the Father turned His back on Him, a sign that God the Father couldn't have anything to do with Him. How can anyone consider the physical, emotional, and spiritual toll that Christ went through a joy?

It was a joy to Him because of the end result of His sufferings. The result was that sin and death were completely and absolutely defeated. The goal was achieved; the victory was won. The even greater joy from Him was that He could have a restored relationship with us—with you.

Lastly, He knew that He'd have a restored relationship with the Father and would take His rightful place in the throne room of heaven. Jesus saw that His sufferings would produce outcomes greater than His suffering: salvation, a restored relationship with His creation, and eternity with His people.

Can you say with Christ that you are enduring your suffering with joy? If nothing else rejoice in the fact that as a Christ-follower you will someday see Jesus seated there, "at the right hand of the throne of grace." The ultimate end of your trials in this world ends in Christ's magnificent presence.

SACRIFICE OF ALL

"But she out of her poverty put in all she had to live on" ~Luke 21:4

Bear with me for a few minutes while I tell you a story. It is a true story involving Jesus and a poor widow. Imagine with me for a moment this story from Luke 21. The setting is Jerusalem, two thousand years ago.

An old wooden door creaks open. Out of the dark small room walks a widow, huddled over, shuffling her feet through the narrow, busy, dirty streets of Jerusalem. On her wrinkled, weathered face are bright eyes and a large smile. This is her weekly march to the Temple to worship the Lord. It's not a long walk, but for her frail body it's a tough one. She climbs the steep Temple steps, out of breath and sweating in the midday sun. Few take notice of her as the city goes about its daily activities.

As she enters the Temple platform she does not focus on the crowds but heads toward the Temple to give her offering. Off in the distance she doesn't notice Jesus, but He notices her.

He sits in the shade of the Temple, surrounded by people listening to His teaching, surrounded by Temple priests ready to pounce on what He says and question His claim of being the Messiah. He pauses from talking to catch His breath and notices the widow slowly making her way to the temple offering stands.

Quietly and solemnly she nears one of the many Temple offering stands, a place to give money to the Temple in honor of the Lord. Around the nearest stand is a group of people tossing their coins into the metal stand. The louder the clang of coins, the more attention and prestige people get and the better they look to those watching. A group of observers encircled the stand, amazed at the generosity of the wealthy.

She slowly walks toward the crowd. The crowd steps back, because they don't want to be seen with such a poor person, especially a widow, someone to be despised. She takes out of her small, leather bag two small coins, the smallest coins available to anyone—like a penny. It is all she has. She rubs the coins together, thinking of what she could do with them. She knows she has no other money, no financial security, and is unsure of her future. As she closes her eyes to briefly pray before dropping her coins into the stand, she thanks the Lord for His presence in her life and His provision for her daily needs. She communicates her trust in the Lord, acknowledging her belief that He will provide. Her offering barely makes a sound as it drops into the box. She turns to walk away.

Jesus watches this quick interchange between the wealthy group of people and the widow. He draws attention to what He just saw to the crowd and says, "Truly, I tell you, this poor widow has put in more than all of them. For all contributed out of their abundance, but she out of her poverty put in all she had to live on."

Like this widow, in our trials we are experiencing some kind of poverty. It may not be poverty of finances, but trials are a loss of something, and it could mean the loss of something great. You and I have stood around that offering stand in our trials as people watched us. We stood there with our eyes closed, praying.

Jesus challenges us as to whether we will allow Him to work as He wills. We must stand there and either trust God with everything we have and everything we are, or we must turn and walk away. That is the choice we have in our trials. This widowed woman was of no significance to the crowds of the Temple. It didn't matter to her though; she knew she was significant to the Lord—not because of anything she did, but because of the nature and character of God.

LANGUISHING

"Be gracious to me, O LORD, for I am languishing; heal me, O LORD, for my bones
are troubled. My soul also is greatly troubled.
But you, O LORD—how long? Turn, O LORD, deliver my life; save me for the sake
of your steadfast love…. The LORD has heard my plea;
the LORD accepts my prayer" ~Psalm 6:2–4, 9

Does this describe where you are right now? Languishing, bones aching, soul troubled? You ask how long; you ask to be delivered. You may be praying this with every heartbeat—down to the depths of your soul. There is no way around it; this is hard, and it's taking all you have just to breathe. Yet, hopefully, you see God as gracious.

The truth of the matter is, you most likely believe that God is going to act according to His will in your life, and as hard as it is right now, God is giving you His best, and all will turn out for your good and for His glory. Those aren't easy thoughts, even on the best of days. Even when every joint and muscle hurts, God will remain faithful, and like He did with David, the psalm writer, God is going to deliver you. He will save you for the sake of His steadfast love. He has made collective promises to His followers through His presence, His Word, and His faithfulness to each of His children. He's also promised future hope in our presence with Him in heaven. He is going to see to it that all of His promises are fulfilled. No promise of God has ever gone unfilled; He is a God of His Word: what He promises He will fulfill—in His timing and by His hand. God, Himself, does not know the word *failure*, because He cannot fail; it goes against everything He is.

"The Lord has heard my plea;
the LORD accepts my prayer" (*Psalm 6:9*)

At the end of the psalm we see how God answered David. God heard David's plea, and the Lord accepted his prayer. You may feel right now that God is being silent, that He has removed His presence from you. Don't believe it! God hears your every cry, every moan, every plea. He will answer in His time. Remember that the Lord works on a different timetable than we do. And unlike modern conversation (where it's polite to give an immediate answer), God will answer when He feels it's appropriate, when His answer will be most effective. Be encouraged that every prayer, every sound from your soul, is heard by the Savior. Your prayers are never dismissed or disregarded, but the Lord takes to heart every single word. He is listening to you, waiting until His will can best be administered. He will answer.

When Christ was on the cross and cried out, "Father, why have you forsaken me?" the Lord had to turn His back on Christ because of our sin; Christ took our sin upon Himself so you and I could have salvation. God isn't turning His back on you, and He isn't ignoring your cries for mercy, because, as a Christ-follower, you are His. He hears and remembers each plea, and He will answer each one in accordance with His will and greater plan.

In verse 3, David cries, "How long, O LORD?" No doubt David was hoping his trial would be short—just as yours will be. I know I prayed that many times. David had his own doubts or questions about his trial, just like you probably do. Yet just a few verses later, in verse 9, God answers him. David says, "The LORD has heard my plea." We don't know the length of time between verses 3 and 9 in David's life, but just as you cry out to Him now, God is going to bless you with your own verse 9! He will answer you with His mercy and grace, doing good to you at all times.

Just as David did, at some point in your trial you will declare: "The LORD has heard my plea, the LORD accepts my prayer."

OVERCOME THE WORLD

"I have said these things to you, that in me you may have peace.
In the world you will have tribulation.
But take heart; I have overcome the world" ~John 16:33

In its history, our world has had but few years of true peace, and in your trial, there have been few days of peace, if any at all. Jesus, like His entire mission on earth did, directs us to Himself. It is in Him that we find peace in this world. We may pretend to find peace and security in our position, our marriage, our bank account, our possessions, or our expectations, but they are just that, illusions—things that cannot deliver what we think they can promise. All those things are fleeting and passing; they do not last. True peace and contentment is in Jesus Christ alone, it is not in anything or anyone.

How can you have peace in Him though? How do you know that He will be your peace? How can you be reassured of that when peace seems so distant?

Christ says Himself that He's overcome the world. Rest in the truth that in overcoming the world, He gives you peace. He's conquered everything you could ever suffer. You can trust Him, because He's fulfilled what He came to do as your Savior. Your salvation as a Christ-follower is complete. You are secure in your eternal place with Jesus. That cannot be taken away from you, no matter what the world throws at you. In overcoming the world, He secured your place with Him—forever.

When discussing peace, it's strange to see that Jesus says in the same passage, "You will have tribulation." He's talking about peace first, and then He talks about struggle, as the two are connected. He promises peace just as He promises tribulation. As a Christ-follower, you can have peace in your tribulation.

In dying for our sins and resurrecting from the dead, Jesus overcame every aspect of sin and tribulation in the world. He did so willingly. He did so for you. It is He who controls your struggles, your suffering in these dark times. He directed your life along this path, and He will direct your life to its completion. Not that He delights in your trial, but remember the greater good that comes from knowing and trusting Him throughout your life. The world is His, and sin no longer rules it. Every part of this world is under His power and control. Not one thing happens that He is unaware of, including your troubles.

Will you allow peace in your tribulation? Christ is ready to give you peace, no matter the circumstances you face in this world. He has overcome it all, and in Him, so will you.

AS A GOOD SOLDIER

"Share in suffering as a good soldier of Christ Jesus.
No soldier gets entangled in civilian pursuits,
his aim is to please the one who enlisted him" ~2 Timothy 2:3–4

If you have been in the military, you know what it's like to be a soldier, but most of us do not have that experience to relate to. A soldier fights hard and is willing to put everything on the line, including his or her life, for the sake of something greater—such as his or her country, fellow soldiers, or family. In your trial, you are fighting as a soldier would.

Christ is calling you to be sacrificial; He is asking you to abandon something. Your sufferings are different from Christ's (all of our sufferings are different from each other's), but He knows you, and you share in His suffering. Christ is suffering alongside you.

You share this suffering with Christ, and your aim, just as Christ's was, is to please the Lord. The road ahead might be long and difficult. It may be hard to keep your aim on pleasing the Lord at this time, but do the best you can, just as any soldier in combat would do.

Christ called you into your present suffering. Is your aim to please Him?

NONE CAN BE THWARTED

*"I had heard of you by the hearing of the ear,
but now my eye sees you" ~Job 42:5*

Job was someone who received perspective in his trial. He never knew the entire purpose of his great suffering, and most likely, neither will we in ours. We can certainly speculate as to the exact purposes of our trial—just like Job and his friends did—ultimately it comes down to the Lord and His purposes, and we need to be content and joyful in that truth.

By the end of the book of Job, we see how God allowed Job to go through the trial of losing nearly everything. He still had his wife, but he had lost his possessions, his ten children, his standing in the community, and in the end, his friends. He and his friends discussed in great detail the possible reasons for Job's suffering, and even Job questioned his situation. He allowed Himself to ask, "Why?" They also discussed their perceived nature of God. When God entered the narrative in chapter 38, Job had been humbled. God showed Job who He was. Job was able to see God's hand in this world and was also able to see God as God was, not as he *thought* God was. God displayed His majesty to Job, and Job was humbled.

The last words we hear from Job in all of history pertain to his newfound glimpse of God's greatness. He says, "I know that you can do all things, and that no purpose of yours can be thwarted." (*Job 42:1*) Later he says to the Lord, "I heard of you by the hearing of the ear, but now my eye sees You." Job realized that God had a purpose in his suffering, just as He does in ours: it is all about God—seeing God as He is and clinging to Him.

Like Job, your pain will end. And I pray that, like Job, you will have the same perspective: "but now my eye sees you."

Are you open to allowing God to give you a fresh perspective of who He is and how He works? Is it the desire of your life to see Him work in your life, despite the difficulties?

CHOSEN

"You are my servant, I have chosen you and not cast you off;
fear not, for I am with you; be not dismayed, for I am your God;
I will strengthen you, I will help you,
I will uphold you with my righteous right hand" ~Isaiah 41:9–10

The book of Isaiah holds some absolutely incredible truths for you to take hold of and never let go of. The truth of this verse is a gem that I have come back to again and again.

Remember that we did not first choose Jesus in our salvation, but He chose us. And God says here, "I have chosen you." In our sin we would never choose to be saved. The God of the universe looked upon you, wanted you, sought you, claimed you, and died so that He could spend eternity with you. It is His great privilege and delight to walk with you throughout your life. (This sets Christianity apart from all other religions. Outside of biblical Christianity, you supposedly work your way to your god. Only in Christianity has God worked His way to you—not for religion, but for a relationship. God wants to know you and wants you to know Him!)

He directed each step of your life: the exact date and time you were born, where you lived, your education, your job—absolutely everything about you. There is not a second of your life when He is unaware of your plight, not a second He doesn't understand, and not a second of your life that is out of His control. Actually, He knows your life better than you do. And in all of that—the good and the bad of your life, sin included—God chose you.

He directed this trial into your life. He's been right next to you the entire time, and He will remain there, in the sun and in the storm, until the day He takes you home.

God has not left you alone in this trial, and He never will, no matter where the path of suffering takes you. His hand is so upon your life that you cannot turn left or right or take even a simple breath without His allowing you to do so. In this trial it is He who will provide you with strength to endure. It is He who will help you every single step of the way. It is He who will uphold you.

There is nothing to fear when you are in the arms of the Lord. In the reading of His Word, are you realizing God's character—how He works? Are you resting in His sovereignty over your life?

PETER WALKED ON WATER

"He said, 'Come.' So Peter got out of the boat and walked on the water and came to Jesus" ~Matthew 14:29

This really should be titled, "Jesus Walked on Water," but does it really surprise you that Jesus walked on water? He healed the sick, helped the blind see, raised the dead, fed thousands, raised Himself from the dead, and sat Himself at the right hand of God. So it's really no surprise that He could do the miraculous—walk on water. And yes, at his ascension to heaven, He even flew. Christ Himself is absolutely mouth-dropping incredible!

The amazing thing here was that in Christ's power, *Peter* walked on water. After a long day, spent with great crowds, Jesus sent the disciples off in a boat to meet Him on the other side of the Sea of Galilee. Jesus was letting them journey while He went off to pray. (And yes, Jesus prayed!) The disciples were well into the trip across Galilee when Peter looked out and saw a man walking on the water toward them. Land was far away, so of course the disciples were frightened. Peter, scared like the others, inquired as to the identity of the man. He thought it was Jesus, but he wasn't quite sure. He said, "Lord, if it is you, command me to come to you on the water."

Jesus answered, "Come." Peter got out of the boat in faith, while the other eleven stayed behind in the boat.

The rest of the event from Matthew 14 was that Peter got scared, lost faith in Christ, and sank into the water. His faith in Christ faltered, but Christ was always by His side. With each step Peter took, Christ was there ready to catch him.

Your calling is just like Peter's: to leave the comforts of the boat and to walk toward Christ. In many ways, Christ is asking you to leave behind the ease of this life, to go somewhere you've never gone, in order to bring you closer to Himself. Like Peter, your faith may waver and fail, but Christ will always be there to catch you.

Christ's calling to Peter to walk on water was unique to him. None of the other disciples were called out of the boat, only Peter. Just like Peter, in your trial, God is calling you to do something unique—something that only you and Christ can do. Yes, it's hard, and you may fail, but God is calling you out of the boat to do His will and to show His power and glory. But with Him to guide and support you, how can you fail?

Will you surrender to His calling you out of the boat into the stormy waters? Only then can you meet Him, and only then can He work.

NO STING, NO VICTORY

"O death, where is your victory?
O death, where is your sting?" ~1 Corinthians 15:55

Death is a scary prospect that we will all face. It awaits all of us, involves all of us, and comes when we do not want it to. We cannot talk with those who've taken this path before us, because it's a one-way journey, one person at a time, as the Lord wills. (No one goes to heaven and returns to speak about it. If you go to heaven, why would you want to come back? The glory of heaven can't be put into words.) Yet, as Paul writes to the churches in Corinth, he encourages them that death truly has no power over us—none at all.

Something we all fear, death, has no victory, no sting. For the Christian, the act of dying is victory for Christ, because we get to see His work enacted and completed. In dying, the sanctification process is done and moves us on to glorification in eternity. In trusting Christ, especially in our present struggles, we are telling death there is no finality to it. Christ has gone before us for our total victory in His name. It is Christ who has the power, not death. Death has not numbered our days, Christ has, and as Christ-followers, we should rest in that fact. Even in our deaths, Christ is in control.

He has beaten death. Yes, at some point we will physically die, but in Christ, all we have is life. Death is no longer a part of our eternal vocabulary.

TO THE LORD – LIFE OR DEATH

"For if we live, we live to the Lord, and if we die, we die to the Lord. So then, whether we live or whether we die, we are the Lord's" ~Romans 14:8

Some of you are facing a trial that will claim your life, and some of you are facing a trial that will someday end, and you'll have many more years of life ahead. The reality of your life is that you will die—all of us will die. However, whether you live or die, as a Christ-follower you are secure in the Lord's hand. Nothing happens without the Lord's involvement and allowance.

The encouragement of the Apostle Paul in the passage from Romans is that whatever situation you find yourself, in Christ, you are the Lord's, and as the Lord's, you have the ability—in any situation—to live for Him. It's absolutely amazing to know that whatever dire circumstances you face—life or death—you are His and belong to Him. It's the strength you need to continue each day, trusting in Him as you walk down some very treacherous roads. In His presence He gives you the ability to live in and for Him. Those who aren't saved are asking "why" about their situation; they have no direction beyond worldly wisdom, which is no wisdom at all. Our lives in Christ are so much more than our lives in this world.

What a gift it is to live to the Lord, and what a greater gift it is to die to the Lord. As a Christ-follower, you are the Lord's, you belong to no other. Remember that the best is always yet to come—in life and in death.

BLESSED IS THE MAN

"Blessed is the man who remains steadfast under trial, for when he has stood the test he will receive the crown of life, which God has promised to those who love him" ~James 1:12

Do you ever find yourself anxious or wanting to give up—tempted to throw your hands in the air and say, "Enough is enough. I'm done?" God knows those moments when you're done, when you've had it, when you throw your hands in the air in surrender to the trial. My prayer is that you have seen the presence of God in your fight. James writes to us that there is great reward in holding on to the Lord during these dark, difficult days. Part of God's reward and blessing is the trial itself. It's you and God on a dangerous road. You get to see His power and presence, unlike so many others who have no experience with trials or who choose not to embrace God's plan and purpose for them in trials. That alone is enough of a blessing—to see God work in miraculous ways. It's that motivation to see God work that should keep us going.

God's presence may be the only blessing you can see in the trials of this life, and it's the greatest blessing. God promises blessing and reward into eternity, and hopefully you'll see that the greatest blessings are yet to be. The Bible is fairly silent on heaven, on the various crowns the Lord will gift to you, or on what eternal life looks like; however, the best part is that you will be with Him, and that alone is a reward greater than any you could ever imagine. However, your trial and your steadfastness will figure into this life and the greater life to come. God promises His blessing, His presence, and His reward to you—just remain steadfast!

In your struggles, will you desire to remain steadfast in your walk with the Lord, pressing on toward that which the Lord has called you to?

SOLDIER, ATHLETE, FARMER

"No soldier gets entangled in civilian pursuits, since his aim is to please the one who enlisted him. An athlete is not crowned unless he competes according to the rules. It is the hardworking farmer who ought to have the first share of the crops" ~2 Timothy 2:4–6

Paul mentions in this passage three different occupations, or pursuits, in this life: soldier, athlete, farmer. Each is so very different, but Paul finds similarity in them and in the benefit of reviewing them for our Christian life. Each is also not an easy job. Jesus, Paul, and the other authors of the Bible never said the Christian life was going to be easy. Paul is not talking about every reality of these jobs, nor is he discrediting our work if we don't hold to these positions. Each of these roles fits into our overall Christian life—and also into our struggles.

Soldier – The soldier is not a civilian, and his or her life has a different role and purpose than a civilian's does. As a whole, we might say that civilians are less focused and less purposed than soldiers. Civilians have jobs and responsibilities, but life is much more carefree for the civilian: life is often filled with fun and games, and its purpose is, many times, fairly shallow. The soldier cannot do whatever he or she wants. Someone above that individual directs his or her life, and the soldier is required to do what his or her commander orders. The question for us as Christ-followers is: Are we civilians, or are we soldiers?

Athlete – Every four years we get to watch the world's best athletes compete for gold in the Olympics. Most of us are probably athletic, but we can all admit that these athletes are in a class all their own. As a Christ-follower, you are competing in the Olympic games of life. In this passage, Paul draws our attention to the fact that the athlete didn't make the rules; the organization that created the games wrote the rules. For our own "personal Olympic games," who is organizing them? The reality is that God is, and we must live according to His rules. Mankind's problem since the dawn of time is that we've wanted to live according to our own rules, not the rules that were established before creation. As in the Olympic games, the athletes don't tell the organizer how to do things; the organizer tells the athletes how to compete.

I had to ask myself, and still continue to do so: Am I living my life as a Christ-follower as God has directed me? I pray that you will ask yourself that question and fight for obedience to God's Word, no matter the circumstances.

Farmer – The farmer prepares the soil, plants the seeds, cares for the growing crops, and eventually enjoys the harvest. The thing that stands out from Paul's use of the farmer is that in our trials we are planting seeds, hopefully of faith, into the lives of people we meet, talk with, and pray for. In the Christian life we may play different roles that relate to the farmer. We may be preparing soil, planting seeds, encouraging crops to grow, or seeing the harvest bear its fruit. We rarely know the role we play, nor will we ever see the whole picture, but we get to play a part in the farm of God. In the midst of our trials we can live this life of spreading the seeds of the gospel wherever we go. It really doesn't matter what role of the farmer we play. What matters is that we seek the kingdom of God, which means growing the kingdom.

Contemplate of the promise of verse 7: "Think over what I say, for the Lord will give you understanding in everything." The first key word of this verse is to think, to dwell, to ponder the writings of Paul in the Word, as well as the entirety of the Bible. We often do not understand the intricacies of life. Here Paul says that we will have understanding in everything. As a soldier, athlete, and farmer in our trials, we will understand what we need to do—the requirements God has for us as Christians. But Paul doesn't give us a timetable. We may understand aspects of our current suffering, but the reality is that we will not understand it all entirely, at least not yet. When we get to heaven, we will see more clearly what Christ was doing during this time, and then we will understand.

DEFINED BY CHRIST

"I have been crucified with Christ. It is no longer I who live, but Christ who lives in me. And the life I now live in the flesh I live by faith in the Son of God, who loved me and gave himself for me" ~Galatians 2:20

I never imagined that I would have cancer, just as you did not imagine your own suffering. Those who had cancer were a community of people I knew nothing about, and I will admit that I was content in knowing very little of cancer. It was a struggle for others, which I observed from a distance, but this was certainly not for me—nor in my mind would it ever happen to me. When I was diagnosed, a variety of people who had had cancer or had been deeply affected by cancer came forth. In the discussions I had with people, I saw and read about all kinds of perspectives on life—some honored Christ; some did not. There were some who were completely devoted to ridding the world of cancer (a noble and worthy pursuit). There were some who gave advice on what worked for them: such as healthy eating, fitness, or unusual treatments that were unproven. Others exhibited and declared such incredible encouragement. Life changes with this type of diagnosis—as with any trial. You can't go back to living the way you did before. For many, cancer defines their life, whether it's in fighting the cancer or as survivors.

I had to learn through this that my life is not defined by cancer. Yes, cancer is a part of my life and will be for the rest of my life. Yes, my life will never be like it was before. I can't go back to the naïve, ignorant, and somewhat carefree life I had. In fact, my life has been profoundly and forever changed because of the cancer. But our trials do not define us; Christ does. It is in Him that you and I find life and breath and strength.

Hopefully, your identity does not lie in this world, your job, where you live, your family or friends, your country, your bank account, your possessions, and certainly not your trial. As a Christ-follower, your identity lies only in Christ. The key is that your trial is temporary; it is not everlasting. As a child of God, you can be assured that it will end.

My prayer for you is that you are striving to become more like Him, and in Him you will find the most glorious identity and destiny. Put on His identity as opposed to the identity of this world. He (not your trial) is your existence and definition.

Christ has defined you in calling you to be His child. He has laid claim to you; He has sealed you with His Spirit. In all ways—in every up and down you will ever go through—you are His, and your name belongs to Him. The only thing you need to live out is the identity of Christ

GRACE FOR THE ABSENT

"If one member suffers, all suffer together; if one member is honored, all rejoice together" ~1 Corinthians 12:26

Not everyone you know is willing to walk this journey with you. Some are scared for you (or themselves); some are really, really "busy," and others are only along for the ride, and when the ride gets rough they leave. Sometimes it's hard having to walk alone, without those you thought would walk in the darkness with you. Remember that God is working in their lives just as much as He is in yours. Just like us, they have a lot to learn.

When talking about those who are on this journey and those who are not, remember that life goes on for those who are not directly involved. Your life may have stopped, but for everyone else, life continues on, as it always has. As life goes on for almost everyone you know, give some grace to those who are unable to, or choose not to, join you and walk this path of pain with you. Remember, they may not be physically present, but they may be desperately praying for you. Yes, they missed out on the learning and the joys of walking this road with you, and yes, it may be frustrating and sad, it's okay to feel bad for them. But forgive them where forgiveness is needed.

One thing that amazed me in my own trial were people that I had no idea were praying for me or that were even on this journey with me, even if from a distance. Even over a year afterward, I found out about people who had been praying. And remember: if you think no one is praying, I am praying and entreating your cause to the Lord each day. As Christ-followers we are called to walk this life together, to encourage each other, exhort each other, and be the iron that sharpens iron. (*Proverbs 27:17*) By the Lord's grace and wisdom, others will someday learn firsthand what it's like to walk through trials, and you, through the grace God provides, will get to show them the love of Christ.

As Christ-followers, we are called to suffer and rejoice together. Paul doesn't qualify the suffering and rejoicing; he only states that we as the church are to do both—as one. It's easy for us to rejoice together over the good things that happen in our lives. It's much harder to suffer together. It requires vulnerability and transparency that few are willing to make. But Paul writes that we are to walk this road of life together. At some point in this journey of darkness, the church will recognize what God has done. Luke writes in Acts 14:27: "And when they arrived and gathered the church together, they declared all that God had done with them, and how he had opened a door of faith to the Gentiles."

God is doing good in your life right now, and He is opening a door for you to share your faith with unbelievers.

LEAD THE LIFE

"Only let each person lead the life that the Lord assigned to him, and to which God has called him" ~1 Corinthians 7:17

Did you choose where you were born or the parents you were born to? Did you choose the time period you were born into? Did you choose your hometown? Did you choose your natural abilities and talents? Did you really choose anything about yourself? The answer is a resounding, "No." And yet, we think we have control of every aspect of our lives. It's a common delusion.

The list goes on and on and on of the things in our lives we have no control over. The reality is that we have a Maker, who, even before the dawn of time, knew where He wanted you to be born, to whom He wanted you to be born to, the exact time period and location for where He wanted you to be born, and the talents you would have. He handcrafted you in His image, as He willed. Everything about you was orchestrated with exact precision by His hand.

God places an individual where He desires for a specific purpose, a specific calling—especially His children. In this, God only asks one thing of us: to live the life He gave us, for His glory.

Christ-follower, God has given us an even greater calling: to serve and glorify Him in any way He sees fit, to proclaim His name to the peoples of this earth, and to seek His kingdom. We may find ourselves in some exciting situations, sharing Christ with others; we may find ourselves in the mundane parts of life, sharing His truth; and we may find ourselves in the valley, trusting Christ. Our lives are those of His choosing, for His ultimate glory and our good benefit.

God knows exactly what you are going through at this very moment. He knew before He created you that you would be going through this hardship. He knew your pain, your suffering, your trial. He knew how hard it would be for you. The amazing thing is that God has called your name to do what you currently are, in whatever circumstance you have no control over. Just as He called me to have cancer, He called you to your hardship. In creating you, God knew the ups and downs of your life, the highest mountaintops and deepest valleys. He knew each sin, each harsh word, and each question you have had of Him. Yet, He still chose to create you and to pursue you for salvation in Him.

Take a moment and think about what you just read. The God of the entire universe wrote your life story and called you to live the life you're living. No one else in all of history could live your life. It's not about strength in enduring a trial, but about the fact that God didn't call anyone else to live your life or to go through your trial. People may be walking with you at this moment, but only you could live up to this specific calling in your life by His strength and power. Isn't that amazing?

Right now, your trial is your calling. This is what God wants you to do, and God is going to work through you in ways you could never envision. God called Job to suffer so that you could, thousands of years later, read Job's experience and response to suffering. Job never knew you would read his story, yet Job's calling was to suffer for his own benefit—and for yours. Likewise, your calling is one that is beyond your understanding.

God's calling upon your life truly is magnificent. Embrace it, as well as the One who called you to live the life at hand!

THE MISSION IN SUFFERING

"What then shall we say to these things?
If God is for us, who can be against us?" ~Romans 8:31

Most of us are not called by Jesus to leave our homes and go overseas, but we are called to share Jesus with the people the Lord has placed before us in our homes, at our workplaces, in our families—whomever we meet, wherever we go. You could say that we're called to grow where we are planted and to spread seeds of the gospel wherever we go. In your suffering there is a great mission field placed right in your lap. You literally do not need to pursue anyone; they come right to you. Nurses, social workers, family, bankers, friends, coworkers are all there to share Christ with or to encourage in Christ. There may not be an easier mission field than the one the Lord has given you in your suffering, though I know it doesn't always feel that way. In your present darkness, Christ is going to shine brighter than any star in the entire universe.

This devotion by John Piper discusses the specific mission work of Overseas Missionary Fellowship, yet it fits so perfectly with our own mission work in suffering. It is a bold statement to say that suffering is a similar opportunity to the risk many take when going overseas to bring Christ to a dark world. Hopefully, you are already risking it all by trusting God. All God asks of you is that you seek His kingdom and share Him with the people you meet, wherever you are. In your suffering you can be the boldest witness. God is with you in your suffering, and He is also with you as you share His Son—like a great evangelist—to many in need. You may be the only representative of Christ a person may ever meet. Consider how He may use you.

John Piper leaves us with these thoughts in the discussion of being a faithful witness:

> Hudson Taylor put it this way: "There is a living God. He has spoken in the Bible. He means what He says and will do all that He has promised." Lives of faith are the great mirror of the dependability of God.

My prayer for you is that in the hardships you are facing or will face, reflect the light of the Lord better than the moon reflecting the light of the sun. I pray that you will depend wholly upon Him. If God is for us, then no one can be against us.

* * *

http://solidjoys.desiringgod.org/en/devotionals/
dependable-in-the-mundane

THE PARTING WATERS

"When the waters saw you, O God, when the waters saw you, they were afraid;
indeed, the deep trembled. The clouds poured out water; the skies gave forth thunder;
your arrows flashed on every side. The crash of your thunder was in the whirlwind;
your lightnings lighted up the world; the earth trembled and shook. Your way was
through the sea, your path through the great waters;
yet your footprints were unseen. You led your people like a flock
by the hand of Moses and Aaron" ~Psalm 77:16–20

When God enters the scene, anywhere and at any time in history, things get frightening. Frightening, not in the sense of scary, but frightening in the sense of the great things that are going to happen that we may not completely understand. In Psalm 77, the psalmist is remembering the Lord's work in the life of the people of Israel—specifically the Lord's leading the people out of Egypt to start their journey to the Holy Land.

It is amazing to see God work. The psalmist says that the waters are afraid at the sight of the Lord; His lightning lights up the world; the earth trembles and shakes at His command; He spreads the sea unseen and leads His people. The very God that is at work in your life right now is the same God who makes water scared. Wow! The water sees the Lord, and is afraid. Can you think of any nonliving thing that exhibits emotion? Water is not alive, and yet it fears the Lord!

It is the same exact thing in your trial. God is at work, even though you may not see Him. Every answered prayer is God at work. Every breath is God at work. Every encouraging word is God at work. Every message you need to hear at the time you need to hear it is God at work. God is more at work in your life right now than you will ever know. In the storm you are in, God is going to part the waters for you. You will walk through this valley successfully guided by the unseen hand of the Lord. Learn to embrace the truth of God's mighty work in your life. After all, He can make the water afraid of Him. So cool!

BIG GOD, SMALL TRIAL

"Have you not known? Have you not heard? The LORD is the everlasting God, the Creator of the ends of the earth. He does not faint or grow weary; his understanding is unsearchable" ~Isaiah 40:28

We want a god who can fit into our world, our thinking, and our desires. We want a god of our own creation, under our control—a god we can manipulate to our own ends. But in the end, the reality is that we want to be god; that truly is the thread of human history and of every human since the Garden. Even Christians have this same viewpoint, though they may never say or admit it. If God is how we want Him to be than He is very small and incapable of handling our problems. Yet God cannot be controlled or manipulated by anyone or anything. He is not *a god*, but *the God*, not small, but massive (if that word can even describe Him). He is as He is, not as you or I depict Him.

If there is one thing to learn in our troubles, it is that God is larger than any of the problems we may face in this life. We serve a big God, and any trial, any cancer, or any plague is a small problem in His book. It's not small to us, but God is bigger than we are. He is so vast that, this side of heaven, we cannot process Him entirely. It is He who is the only One who can adequately handle any situation. We need a bigger view of God and a smaller view of ourselves and an even smaller view of our trials.

Yet, as big as God is, He cares so deeply for you. Compared to God, we are so small.

SAVOR THE LORD

"The LORD is good to those who wait for him, to the soul who seeks him.
It is good that one should wait quietly for the salvation of the Lord....
Let him sit alone in silence
when it is laid on him" ~Lamentations 3:25–26, 28

The Lord has given each of us a certain number of days. Yours are different from mine. While He calls us to number our days, He also calls us to the quality of our days—meaning, the way we live and how we impact the people around us. The key to fully living the days given to us is to savor the Lord and to savor the time the Lord has given us—every moment. We are called to value our time with the Lord, and whether the times are good or bad, we are the Lord's. Every moment with the Lord must be cherished. And as hard as it is right now, I pray that you cherish the time with Him.

You may find that there are days when you have nothing related to your trial that you need to do, or that your trial isn't a pressing burden for that day. Relish these days of quiet and relative peace. Take life one day at a time; enjoy the day the Lord has made while the day is at hand. Each day is a gift and a great blessing given to you by the Lord.

After I finished six weeks of radiation and chemotherapy, there were a few weeks when I was waiting to find out the next steps for my chemo treatments and for a final diagnosis of the type and grade of cancer I had. The Lord laid it upon my heart to enjoy the time without any treatment. I was still recovering from the radiation and chemo, but what a joy it was not to take any pills—or forget to take pills—or to have my head in a hard plastic mask, locked to a table. You may find that there are days between doctor's appointments or job interviews or your meeting with "that" person. The Lord is giving you these little gifts of rest to renew and strengthen you. It may be a small amount of strength, but it's still strength that you need and that you didn't have before. These are days when you can hopefully enjoy the company of a good friend and a quality conversation, or maybe even a needed diversion like a movie or sleep.

In the midst of trials God always gives some minor respites. Enjoy them while they are there and gear up for whatever may be coming next.

The hardest part of this is to part ways with your worry and anticipation in order to enjoy a time of God-given rest.

TO THE CHURCH

"So then you are no longer strangers and aliens, but you are fellow citizens with the saints and members of the household of God....
In him you also are being built together
into a dwelling place for God by the Spirit" ~Ephesians 2:19–22

The church is a group of people committed to Christ, to His Word, to His kingdom, to His glory, to proclaiming His salvation to the world. At least, that's what the church is supposed to be. Church is so much more than a weekly service, some songs, and a sermon; it is so much more than social hour or checking a box on your to-do list for the weekend. We are not called to live the Christian life alone, but we are called to walk each step in Christ, as the church, together, no matter our age, job, life stage, or relational status. The church is Christ.

When I was diagnosed with cancer, I got a completely new perspective of the church. For me it literally came alive in a way I had never seen. I had always been praying for the people on the church's prayer list, never expecting to be on that list myself, and now I was on the prayer list to be prayed for. I saw a group of people literally get on their knees for the sake of my health and for the glory of the Lord. I saw the hearts of so many thrive as they sought the Lord through my circumstances. This wasn't the whole church, but it was the core of the church—those committed to Christ in every aspect of their lives. Together we were becoming more like Christ.

Along the journey there were some who came alongside for a prayer and some who visited me in the hospital. There was a remarkable group who committed themselves to the entire journey, including the risks and darkness from the beginning to whatever end the Lord may have willed. It was a blessing to know I didn't walk this path alone. There were quite a few things I learned and saw about the church that I could never have imagined if I hadn't walked this road of suffering. The church had a new vibrancy to it—at least it did from my perspective. I saw the church change from just a weekly gathering into a people living out the Bible. Actually, they had always lived out the Bible. Now I saw it for myself.

As the church, we are called to live the Christian life together—the good and the bad, the times of feast and the times of famine, and even the mediocre times of our humdrum lives. We were never meant to walk this path alone. As Paul writes in 1 Corinthians 12:20, "As it is, there are many parts, yet one body." One reason we have the church is to grow together in Christ and to walk at all times of life as one. Paul continues in verse 26: "If one member suffers, all suffer together, if one member is honored, all rejoice together." That is what we are called to do as the body of Christ.

It can be discouraging when the church fails and doesn't come alongside its own people or doesn't fulfill the expectations Christ has for His followers in the church. Remember that the church is filled with people just like you and me; the reality is that we are all hypocrites and sinners in need of Christ and His grace. No one is perfect, and we will all fail at some point in our lives in the church. Sadly, at some point we will fail someone who needs us.

Pray for those who may have failed you on this journey. In some cases, they have failed God and His expectations of them in such circumstances. Pray that they will have an opportunity to learn God's call upon their life through your journey and beyond. It's hard, but there will come a time when we will need to extend a bit of grace and forgiveness to someone and, dare I say, also a bit of grace and forgiveness on ourselves for our own failings.

We live in such a false and plastic world, even in the church. We come to church with our plastic face on and, amazingly, each week everybody is "doing great." This is the weekly reality of the church for most people. The truth of Christian relationships is that we are not to stay on the surface of our souls. God expects us to go deep, to share His truth with each other as we struggle to grow more like Christ, to live in the depths of our souls. It's easy to be shallow in these types of relationships, because we risk almost nothing, and it costs almost nothing from us. To go deep we have to be vulnerable and transparent; we have to take risks in sharing our lives. In our "Fakebook" world it may be that we just don't want to.

In everything, though, God has a greater calling upon our lives than the simplicities and vanities of our twenty-first-century lives. He is calling us to be vulnerable, to ask for prayer, to say we need help, because Christ will work greatest in this type of heart and life. It's a risk, because people may see our weaknesses, and yet the truth is that they will see God's strength working in our weakness.

The last exhortation to the church is for us not to leave when the journey is ended. The journey can be a great time of growth in Christ and with each other, and we could say the same of the recovery from these dark times. The trial may have awakened some relationships, including the strengthening of our relationship with Christ. Keep those relationships after the storm is over. The journey of suffering will end, but the journey toward heaven is the work of Christ and is ongoing until the end. You and I get to walk toward heaven with some incredible believers in Christ. And if we're serious about our faith in Christ, we will joyously walk this journey toward heaven together.

Is your pursuit of the church as strong as your pursuit of Christ? The church is the body of Christ, don't forget that. You need the church, and the church needs you!

HIS PURPOSE

"The LORD will fulfill His purpose for me; your steadfast love, O LORD, endures forever. Do not forsake the work of your hands" ~Psalm 138:8

There is nothing that God does without reason and purpose. Unlike us, He doesn't make rash decisions or act according to His feelings or emotions. Every action, every word, every detail of His is done with an exact plan, and in the end it all works out exactly to His will and desire. You too have reason and purpose in your life. He created you for, and with, a specific calling in mind. Your existence is not a waste, and your trial is not a waste.

God orchestrates our lives in such a way that we play a part in fulfilling His purposes for this world. Our trial plays a part in the greater purposes of the Lord, and the reality is that we may never know the exact reason why we're suffering. There are usually multiple reasons for our suffering and for what God wants to accomplish in our lives.

You never know who is going to be encouraged by your response to your plight, who might grow closer to Christ in your suffering, or even who may come to Christ by seeing your example of faithfulness in your pain. God's purpose in your trial involves so many others—believers and unbelievers alike. The intricacies of our trials, and our lives, are far beyond our understanding.

Trust this though: God will fulfill His ultimate plan and purpose for you, both in this world and in your life. Trust in His divine plan, and His purpose will come to completion. Your purpose on this earth will be fulfilled.

COUNT IT AS LOSS

"But whatever gain I had, I counted as loss for the sake of Christ. Indeed, I count everything as loss because of the surpassing worth of knowing Christ Jesus my Lord. For his sake I have suffered the loss of all things and count them as rubbish, in order that I may gain Christ" ~Philippians 3:7–8

Is there anything on this earth worth losing your livelihood, your family, every comfort, every desire you've ever had? What if you gave up every single thing you owned, your dreams, your ambitions? What would you expect in return for sacrificing everything?

The Apostle Paul faced these exact questions. By the time he wrote to the Philippians, he had lost everything. He sat in a Roman prison, looking over his life, his health, the energy he had spent planting churches and developing relationships, and the letters he had written to his brothers and sisters around the Roman Empire. As he looked over his life, he truly counted it all as loss, but what did he lose, and what did he gain? His perspective could only come through the grace of God.

In the end Paul was willing to give up his life—he was executed by the Romans—for one thing, knowing Christ.

You probably are not in prison having given up everything. Most likely you haven't lost every single thing you own, every freedom or right, every relationship in your life. But Paul had literally lost everything, save for a few faithful friends who came to visit him in his infirmity and in his imprisonment. He had nothing, and he knew the exact path he was on—that of his execution, for being a Christian, no less.

If you were to ask Paul if it was worth it, he would undoubtedly say, "Yes," and he would be ready to do so a thousand times over if that's what the Lord required of him. If it meant even one person being saved, there would be no doubt in his mind that it was all worth it. He saw Christ as more valuable than anything he was holding on to—more valuable than any relationship he ever had on earth.

Paul admitted that it was for Christ that he'd been willing to give up everything. He actually called everything he was holding on to in this world "rubbish." It was all trash compared to gaining Christ.

Do you view your loss like that? Do you see how much greater Christ is than anything or anyone in your life? It's not to say we don't love people; quite the contrary. Paul loved all the churches he founded and ministered to. He loved all the people who worked with him in ministry and those he had never met but were nonetheless, praying for his ministry. No doubt he thought and prayed for them regularly. But compared to Christ there was nothing in this world that was of the same value as Christ.

If you were to add the entire wealth in all of history, it truly is a pittance compared to the wealth of Christ. If you considered the goodness of every relationship you have ever had, ever will have, or ever dreamed of having, it doesn't add up to the value of intimately knowing Jesus Christ.

You see, God wants you. He wants your possessions, your time, your conversations, your relationships, and your dreams. He wants all of you. In this trial He is showing you how to give up this world in exchange for knowing Him. Are you willing?

PRESERVE MY LIFE

"Remember your word to your servant, in which you have made me hope. This is my comfort in my affliction: that your promise gives me life. The insolent utterly deride me, but I do not turn away from your law. When I think of your rules from of old, I take comfort, O LORD. Hot indignation seizes me because of the wicked, who forsake your law. Your statutes have been my songs in the house of my sojourning. I remember your name in the night, O LORD, and keep your law. This blessing has fallen to me, that I have kept your precepts" ~Psalm 119:49–56, NIV

Take a look at this particular writer's plight. He's being falsely accused of something, mocked by the arrogant, and surrounded by the wicked. Each of us at some point is going to receive criticism. It might be our fault, but if we're living fully and daily in Christ, it most likely won't be. The psalmist presents his problem to the Lord and writes about how the Lord is going to act in this particular situation.

It's not that the psalmist is commanding the Lord to work. It's that he is speaking to the Lord about how He has acted in the past, and since God is faithful to His children, He will act. The psalmist realizes that God is going to act in His timing, according to His will, and as He desires. The writer of these verses has no control over how God is going to act, but he knows that God is willing to act. He communicates his trust in God, and to God, through this psalm.

The psalmist starts by asking God to remember His past promises—the past working of His hands. The psalmist is encouraged, because he knows that God has worked in the past, and he has hope because he knows the Lord is going to work this time. He writes of comfort in his suffering because of the promises of God. The promises the psalmist was recalling are the same ones you are reading in the Bible—the exact ones. As God has worked in the past, so He is going to work in your life, that is His promise in your current circumstances.

At night, when he's wide awake, thinking about his situation, the psalmist remembers the name of the Lord, who God is, and how He acts. In the night and in the darkness the psalmist decides to turn to the light. When his mind could be consumed with his own plight, he turns to the Lord and His Word. This brings great comfort, because the Lord has it all under control.

The goal of Psalm 119 is that we would be in the Word of God and act in obedience to God in mind and action. The psalmist remembers God in his suffering and decides to obey God, to follow God's purpose in his life. He starts the passage by saying how God is going to work and recounting the promises God has made. He ends the passage by saying what he's going to do. He will choose to be obedient, no matter his circumstances. The psalmist doesn't say when his trial ends or the outcome of his trial. But in the midst of his trial he is choosing to live in obedience and follow God.

Like the psalmist, in whatever you are facing, will you choose to follow Christ down whatever road or into whatever valley He has for you?

THE LORD IS HIS NAME

"He who made the Pleiades and Orion, and turns deep darkness into the morning and darkens the day into night, who calls for the waters of the sea and pours them out on the surface of the earth, the LORD is his name; who makes destruction flash forth against the strong, so that destruction comes upon the fortress" ~Amos 5:8–9

It's hard to do in the city, and being from LA, I have only done it a few times, but have you ever sat on the grass during summer and looked up to the stars? Have you looked up at the stars and wondered about your own existence—why you are here? What's the purpose in all of this? Our world? Our lives? Our livelihood?

Imagine this: God at the dawn of creation in Genesis 1, talking about the different stars and galaxies He's creating—Pleiades, Orion, Milky Way, Earth. As He calls its name, each comes into existence. It is the same with our so cleverly named star, the sun. Just as He spoke these stars and galaxies into existence, He calls the sun to rise each morning and to set each night. Yes, I know the science of the sunrise and sunset, but the reality is, God is directing the revolutions and rotations of the planets. It's all under His command—each morning and each evening.

Think beyond the big things. What about the winds, the clouds, volcanoes, raindrops? What about the air in our lungs and the cells in our bodies? Does God not control those things also?

How about history? Can He orchestrate events and the movement of people for His purpose? What about your life? Can He orchestrate your life for something beyond yourself? Can you trust Him to orchestrate your own life?

Remind me who we're talking about. Ah yes, I remember,—God, the Lord is His name. Think back to this passage from Amos: He creates the Pleiades, Orion; He turns darkness into light and light into darkness. The Creator of the universe is just as involved in the universe as He is in your life, probably even more.

What is He doing in your life? I pray that you will take some time to see God at work, especially in the circumstances you are currently facing. It may be that He is subtly and quietly working, or it may be that you can see Him working every minute of every day. At this moment you may not see Him working, but look around—all around you. He is working in each heartbeat, breath, sunrise, and sunset. All of it is happening by His hand.

What was His name? "The LORD is His name."

YOU ANSWERED ME

"I thank you that you have answered me
and have become my salvation" ~Psalm 118: 21

In a psalm declaring the endurance of the Lord's steadfast love, there is a reality that God loves to answer prayer. The only problem for us is that so many times it is not answered in the ways we expect or want. The writer does not say that the Lord answered his prayer to meet his expectations, but he says that God answered him, and for that the psalmist is grateful.

There were so many times I prayed for healing from the cancer. Throughout weeks and months of prayer, the reality at the end of the day was that I still had cancer, and the overall healing never came. I still had to go through surgeries, procedures with their complications, chemotherapy, and radiation. At the end of the day, after many hours of prayer, you may still be in your situation.

One of the things I had to learn was that while my big prayer wasn't answered the way I desired, there were all of these small prayers that were being answered—tons of them. I just had to open my eyes to how the Lord was directing His will in my cancer. Some of the answers to prayer were that the doctor had an open appointment, an MRI went smoothly, or that traffic wasn't bad (welcome to L.A.). There were so many prayers that were answered that we were completely unaware of, it was absolutely uplifting to look at all the graces Christ had bestowed to me and my family. Those same graces He will give to you—small, almost imperceptible answers to prayer, but He answers nonetheless.

My family created a Book of Blessings, recording answered prayers during the immediacy of the cancer diagnosis, removal, and treatments. It is filled with small answered prayers that grew our faith in God's ability to control the journey and brought peace and comfort that God had all things under His control. Each time there was an answered prayer, we were eager to document it and rejoice in God's work, even though it wasn't necessarily what we wanted. We held and continue to hold on to God's gracious provisions.

God is working in your life, from the big to the small. I pray that you will open your eyes to the hand of the Lord upon your life.

PURIFYING PATHWAY

"Let us know; let us press on to know the LORD; his going out is sure
as the dawn; he will come to us as the showers,
as the spring rains that water the earth" ~Hosea 6:3

Before you came to Christ in salvation, your entire life was heading
toward an eternity of punishment. It may sound strange, but without
Christ, every day you were getting closer and closer to that punishment.
It was punishment for your sin and avoidance of God. However, when
you come to Christ, you change paths; you were no longer facing eternal
punishment without God, but a new, eternal life, focused on God.

However, your heart is going through a process on this earth called
sanctification. Sanctification is God working in your life to take your
focus off this world and to refocus and repurpose your life for Him and
His work, to make you holy, just as Christ is completely holy.
Essentially, He is working to make you more like Him—more Christlike.
Your sanctification, or becoming like Christ, ends the moment you enter
heaven, but right now, you have to work on becoming more like Christ.
Your efforts do not save you, but are the work of the Spirit in your life
toward a greater life in Christ.

Sanctification is happening each day through a variety of means.
One way God sanctifies and purifies our lives is through trials. As Piper
writes, "The aim of God...is to knock the props out from under our
hearts so that we rely utterly on Him."

No matter how long you've been a Christian, there is always a part
of your heart that is still sinful, still reliant on this world. I hate to break
it to you, but no one is perfect, except Christ. Every Christian has some
area in which he or she is holding on to the things of this world. God is
using your trial to take your heart off this world. He is showing you how
the world has failed you, how only He can provide what you need.

In your trial, God is showing you that you need to rely solely on
Him and not the things of this world. This world—and all the
people in it—will fail you at one time or another. There is one

constant in your life, that constant is Christ. Believer, learn to rely not on yourself, your family, your possessions, or anything else, but on Christ alone.

* * *

http://cdn.desiringgod.org/website_uploads/documents/books/
dont-waste-your-cancer.pdf

MAN IN THE ARENA

"Do you not know that in a race all the runners compete, but only one receives the prize? So run that you may obtain it. Every athlete exercises self-control in all things. They do it to receive a perishable wreath, but we an imperishable. So I do not run aimlessly; I do not box as one beating the air. But I discipline my body and keep it under control, lest after preaching to others I myself should be disqualified" ~1 Corinthians 9:24–27

Known informally as the "Man in the Arena" speech, these words from President Theodore Roosevelt give encouragement to all who face criticism from others and also face the trials of life.

> It is not the critic who counts; not the man who points out how the strong man stumbles, or where the doer of deeds could have done them better. The credit belongs to the man who is actually in the arena, whose face is marred by dust and sweat and blood; who strives valiantly; who errs, who comes short again and again, because there is no effort without error and shortcoming; but who does actually strive to do the deeds; who knows great enthusiasms, the great devotions; who spends himself in a worthy cause; who at the best knows in the end the triumph of high achievement, and who at the worst, if he fails, at least fails while daring greatly, so that his place shall never be with those cold and timid souls who neither know victory nor defeat.

Whatever has befallen you these past months and years, you may be subject to criticism. Think of yourself in the Coliseum or running a marathon. There are few in the arena or running the race. Everyone else is on the sidelines, watching. It's easy for others to criticize and critique your every movement and decision. There may be people who will openly mock you and those who will do so behind your back. Critics are a dime a dozen in this life—as plentiful as the pigeons on a New York City sidewalk. Sadly, there are those plotting and hoping for your demise, sadly some of these are even in the church.

You are among the few chosen to be in the race, to be in the arena, while the world watches on. Some are praying for the Lord's success and for your success also; others are hoping for the Lord's failure and for your utter failure. I dare say that there may even be people praying for your failure.

I hope you find encouragement in the verse from Paul and the excerpt from President Theodore Roosevelt. The critic is a mere bystander. The person who criticizes is not in the stadium of life, as you are, covered in blood and sweat, seemingly broken but not entirely beaten. The job of the critic is easy. It costs nothing, requires no energy, and creates a false sense of pride for him or her. In your suffering there will be missteps, mistakes, and possibly some regrets, but keep doing your best to fight for your faith, trusting in Christ with every step.

Take courage my friend. As Roosevelt says, you are not that "cold and timid soul" like your critic. You know victory, you know defeat, but most of all, you know the work of Jesus in your life. Christ is ultimately victorious over any perilous situation you find yourself in. And it is Christ who will take care of any critic for you. Your race in this life is not yet finished. Press on toward the higher calling of the Lord. Ignore the shouts from the stands and focus on the presence of Jesus.

* * *

http://www.theodore-roosevelt.com/
images/research/speeches/maninthearena.pdf

EQUIPPED TO DO HIS WILL

*"Now may the God of peace who brought again from the dead our Lord Jesus, the great shepherd of the sheep, by the blood of the eternal covenant, equip you with everything good that you may do his will,
working in us that which is pleasing in his sight, through Jesus Christ, to whom be glory forever and ever. Amen" ~Hebrews 13:20–21*

Have you ever truly prayed for God's will? Doing so means that you are putting everything on the line to see God work. You are telling God that everything in your life is at His disposal. You are giving Him complete control over every aspect, every possession, every relationship, and every pursuit. Praying for His will in your life means that you are living day to day, trusting that God will do what He needs to do for the sake of His kingdom and the glory of His name. This may mean that your life will be blessed materially, with great relationships. Or it might mean allowing hardship into your life. Truly this is one of the greatest risks anyone can ever take.

The wonderful thing in praying for God's will is that God is at work. You are allowing and inviting Him to work in your life, though the reality is that He doesn't need your permission to work in your life. He wants to do His greatest good in your life. Therefore, wanting His will is the greatest good in your life, whatever your life may look like with God in control.

In 2012, I prayed for the Lord's will over my life. I felt very much at a crossroads. Life hadn't gone as I had expected, and I gave everything over to the Lord. Even though I enjoyed so many aspects of my life, I was ready for a change. I didn't know what to expect, but I was ready to see God work.

You know the story of how God acted in His will for my life. I did not expect what happened, but I am so thankful for the Lord's will in this way, and I am excited for how He chooses to act in the future. May I dare you to honestly pray the Lord's will for your life? Trust me, you won't be disappointed.

THE POTTER AND THE CLAY

"But now, O LORD, you are our Father, we are the clay, and you are our potter, we are all the work of your hand" ~Isaiah 64:8

Isaiah is giving us an illustration that makes it easy for us to understand God's role and our role, as well as God's power and our power. A potter takes a lump of clay, and with his skilled hands turns it into something useful, something beautiful. We are the work of His hands, not the other way around. God has a purpose for you as His clay; His hands are all over your life. You are a vessel created in His image, as He desires. He put His personal touch into creating us. He is creating and calling you for a specific purpose. You are a beautiful vessel meant to display and reflect the glory of the Lord. The God who made the universe chose each of your characteristics and capabilities. In many ways, you are a practical vessel, enduring the hard and dusty parts of life for a reason and for a purpose. As a Christ-follower, you are to carry His Word and salvation to others as His handcrafted child—the Potter's handiwork.

We need to recognize His control and sovereignty over our lives, the good and the bad. He has it all within His grasp. There are no broken or misshapen clay pots in God's kingdom. Each is a beautiful piece of work in His collection, formed for His use.

Like Christ was poured out on the cross, you too are being poured out in His service and for His glorious purpose.

THE LOVE OF CHRIST

"For God so loved the world, that he gave his only Son, that whoever believes in him should not perish but have eternal life. For God did not send his Son into the world to condemn that world, but in order that the world might be saved through him" ~John 3:16–17

It is hard to think of suffering as an outpouring of love, but God loves you through your situation. Every moment of every day of your journey, the Lord desperately loves you. I have heard this truth quoted often: God loves you more in a minute than any single person could love you in a lifetime. It's hard to grasp the significance of that statement when life hurts so badly, but it is the reality and truth of God's love for His children. God is loving you through this and is right there with you, every step of the way.

One of the amazing things is that in our present suffering, God is preparing us to enjoy Him forever. He is training us to see how great and glorious He is—over anything this world holds and over any pains in this life. One day we will look back on our lives, see the hand of God, and praise the Lord for His presence during each breath of this journey we call life.

John Piper writes: "Jesus Christ is mightily loving His people with omnipotence, moment-by-moment love that does not always move us from calamity but preserves us for everlasting joy in His presence even through suffering and death." In John 3:16–17, Jesus declared His purpose to save the world. Your purpose is to declare His salvation to the world.

* * *

http://solidjoys.desiringgod.org/en/devotionals/
present-and-powerful-love

CALLED AND QUALIFIED

"When they had finished breakfast, Jesus said to Simon Peter, 'Simon, son of John, do you love me more than these?' He said to him, 'Yes, Lord; you know that I love you.' He said to him, 'Feed my lambs'" ~John 21:15

John 21 is a very sobering passage, especially for Peter. The crucifixion was over; Jesus had risen from the dead, and now Jesus and Peter needed to meet. Peter had betrayed Christ, not once, but three times. This was a meeting Peter did not want to have, but it was a meeting that would set Peter on the road for spreading the gospel.

Three times Jesus asked the same question of Peter: "Do you love me?" Three times Peter said, "Yes." With each response Jesus gave him purpose: "Feed my lambs...tend my sheep...feed my sheep." The conversation ended with Jesus saying, "Follow me."

Never again did Peter waver in his faith or in his purpose in Christ, though the challenges he would face increased exponentially over the rest of his life, including his execution on the cross (upside down) for his faith in Christ.

Pastor and author Henry T. Blackaby says, "God does not call the qualified, He qualifies the called." I can guarantee that, depending on your trial, many are telling you how strong you are, or that God chose you because of your strength. I heard it often, and I know people meant well, but the reality in my trial of cancer was that I wasn't strong; I couldn't do on my own what the Lord called me to do. There were so many times in the quiet of my soul that I cried, was scared, was in pain, just didn't want to continue on. After each radiation and chemo treatment, lying on the couch doing nothing, I felt like all the strength had left me. I shouted to the Lord, "I can't do this." The reality was that it wasn't any strength within myself that helped me continue on. I was out of strength.

Think about Blackaby's quotation though. God doesn't call the strong because they're strong nor the weak because they are weak. He calls them for His will and purpose, then equips them for His work.

He's calling you because of His plan, and however you fit into His plan, He's going to give you the strength and talent to fulfill your role in that plan, to bring the fruit of the gospel, to help bring people to Him, and to seek and spread His kingdom.

You are only qualified to fulfill His call because of Him—no other reason. As Jesus qualified Peter, He is also qualifying you for the purposes He has for you.

BURDENED BEYOND BELIEF

"For we do not want you to be ignorant, brothers, of the affliction we experienced in Asia. For we were so utterly burdened beyond our strength that we despaired of life itself. Indeed, we felt that we had received the sentence of death. But that was to make us rely not on ourselves but on God who raises the dead" ~2 Corinthians 1:8–9

Some of you have sat in the doctor's office to hear a prognosis that limits your time on this earth. Deep down you already know that God has numbered your days, but for the first time you actually know the number of days you have—if not exact days, within months or a few years. I know how that is, because at one point in my diagnosis I was given just a few years on this earth (this was later changed to an unknown number of years). This is one of those moments, among many in your trial, where you may be burdened beyond your strength. You may have been encumbered by a diagnosis, by your boss letting you go, by that family member or friend saying it's over, by a financial crisis— the list of reasons for suffering goes on. Those burdens are hard to handle, and in those moments you may feel completely powerless, as if there is not enough strength in the entire world.

After hearing a doctor say that your time is limited, you lie awake that night, wondering about everything: your past, your present, and whatever future lies ahead. Paul spent many nights awake and stirring, wondering what would come next, what God was doing. He had the same thoughts that you might have. He, and so many other Christ-followers, have been burdened beyond understanding in their walks with Christ. God never promised a life of ease for the Christ-follower. You've probably sat there praying Jesus would return so that it would all be over, and you would be with Him.

Paul wanted to see purpose in everything God did. He provided us purpose in verse 9 though. He wrote that our trials were "to make us rely not on ourselves but on God who raises the dead." The goal is for you to rely not on any strength, abilities, or talents you may have. The goal is to take your eyes off yourself and this world and to place them squarely on the Lord, who, by the way, has the power to bring life to the dead. As if relying on God wasn't enough, Paul went on to mention the great strength and power of God. In your suffering you feel like dying, like giving up, and here Paul said that you do not have it in you to fight this fight by yourself. You need someone bigger, stronger, and far greater in your trial than yourself or any person on this earth. The one to come to your aid is Jesus. You may not think you will fail yourself, but to be honest, each of us fails, every single day.

Rely on the One who will not fail you in any way or at any time. Rely on Him, Christ-follower. He will respond in grace and love toward you, and in His arms is comfort beyond compare.

BLIND PURPOSE

"But that the works of God might be displayed in him" ~John 9: 3

In John 9, Jesus met a blind man, someone who was born blind and had never seen for a single moment of his life. After meeting the man, the disciples questioned Jesus—more from confusion than anything else. They asked, in verse 2, why the man was blind. Was it the man's sin or his parents' sin? They were wrongly thinking that all trials in life were caused by sin.

The reality was that there was no direct connection between sin and the man's blindness here, and most likely, sin is not the direct cause of your tribulation. Jesus responded, "It was not that this man sinned, or his parents, but that the works of God might be displayed in Him."

This man was chosen from the dawn of creation for this exact encounter with Jesus and His disciples. Your trial is to display the work of God before a dark and unbelieving world. See the glory and handiwork of the Lord in your trial.

This man's trial was given to him to bring glory to God, and what great purpose there will be in your own trial! Later in the passage the religious authorities questioned Jesus, the blind man, and his family regarding the man's blindness and miraculous gift of sight. Their true desire was to discredit Jesus as the Son of God. When asked, the parents replied that their son was old enough and smart enough to answer on his own. The man then responded in verse 25, "One thing I do know, that though I was blind, now I see."

The formerly blind man was speaking such a beautiful truth, though he didn't really know who Jesus was. The man was blind, but now he could see. Isn't that your story too? In your trial you are hopefully going to realize, even if you are saved, that you were blind, and now you see God with more beautiful vision than ever before.

You see life like you have never seen it: in brilliant, vibrant, living color. Just as this man was given new sights, you've been given a new perspective on living.

You are not going to understand every distinct purpose of your trial, but I pray that you will trust in the Lord, and that you will have, in the sight of the Lord, blind purpose—a great purpose in your suffering.

MANY WITNESSES

"Fight the good fight of the faith. Take hold of the eternal life to which you were called and about which you made the good confession in the presence of many witnesses" ~1 Timothy 6:12

This journey is not just your own. It is also the journey of many others—some who are ministering to you, but also many who are observing you. You have yet to see how God is going to use your trial for the benefit of others; and the reality is that you may not see in your lifetime all that God has done through your trial or who was changed because of it. Each person you meet on this journey has an opportunity to see Christ and His salvation shine in you and through you. My prayer is that you will embrace that noble responsibility. Prayerfully you will take up the mantle of evangelism through your interactions with your brothers and sisters in Christ and with those yet to be saved. This trial is so much bigger than you.

One reality is that your life and your faith are on trial in this journey. There may be people who hope you sink and others who hope you sail. There are a great cloud of witnesses, like in Hebrews 11, who are looking to you to see if your faith is true and genuine or if it is merely a moralistic way to live. For some who are observing you, if you fail they may not believe in Christ, but if you succeed, it may help them turn to Christ for salvation.

The choice is yours. Are you going to embrace your trial and show others your Lord through your good confession? Others are watching you; their faith may depend on how they see you trust God in your trial.

THE GOD WHO WORKS

"I will remember the deeds of the LORD; yes, I will remember your wonders of old. I will ponder all your work, and meditate on your mighty deeds. Your way, O God, is holy. What god is great like our God?
You are the God who works wonders; you have made known your might among the peoples. You with your arm redeemed your people, the children of Jacob and Joseph" ~Psalm 77:11–15

All of Psalm 77 is beautiful and holds some great truth for us in these dark times. The words in the first nine verses are words you may have said to yourself. You cry to God, you seek God, you are troubled, you feel as if you are all alone, and you might question God.

When life doesn't make sense we so often lose focus and make claims we don't really intend to make, especially about God. We have all had times when we have felt that we were in this battle alone—as if everyone, including God, had abandoned us. The psalmist feels the same way as he writes.

"Where is God when I've sought Him all the day long? I'm still in the midst of tribulation; why hasn't He come to my aid?" We ask these things in our hearts, but there is always something that causes us to remember God. As verse 10 says, "I will appeal to this, to the years of the right hand of the Most High." The psalmist is astounded when he recalls God's work in the past. It may be hard to remember God's work in your past while you are so focused on your present circumstances, but take a look at the Word of God and how God worked within His people and the church in the past. God has been at work in this world since its creation, and He's been at work in your life since before creation. Remember, remember, remember!

The psalmist, in verses 11–15, takes the time to talk to himself and remind himself of God. Compared with the greatness and majesty of God, our view of God is very small, and the psalmist has to tell himself again and again the truth of God's nature and character, and we need to do the same. He remembers God's handiwork, His mighty deeds, His holiness, the wonders of God's workmanship, and the redemption of the Lord. Having a correct and true view of the Lord will make all the difference in your journey. The only way to know the true God is through His glorious Word.

A right view of God will give you a right perspective of your trial, and you will be victorious in whatever you face.

SUSTENANCE AND RESTORATION

"The LORD sustains him on his sickbed; in his illness you restore him to full health" ~Psalm 41:3

Is the psalmist talking about physical health or spiritual health here? Don't sick people die? So how are they restored? Notice that the person who is sick in this passage is restored to full health during his sickness, not after his sickness. The truth is that he was sustained in his faith by the scriptures, by an encouraging word, by the presence and prayers of a faithful friend.

The Lord gives all the provision needed for robust spiritual health while in the ICU, in the courtroom, in the doctor's waiting room, or anywhere you are. His Spirit is present to give you the strength to continue on. Wherever you are suffering, know that Christ will give you everything you need to be strong in Him.

Full health may not mean physical healing; it may not mean financial prosperity or a new job. The full health the psalmist writes about has nothing to do with the material or physical things in this world. God is greatly concerned about your lot in this life, but even more so He is concerned with your spiritual health and how you are trusting in Him.

Only in heaven will we have a complete, full healing, with full health. As hard as it is to think about our passing, doesn't full spiritual healing sound wonderful?

REJOICE IN CHRIST

"But rejoice insofar as you share Christ's sufferings, that you may also rejoice and be glad when His glory is revealed" ~1 Peter 4:13

While each trial is unique, you may find that many people will try to relate to your suffering, and there will be many who can relate. It's natural for us to try to understand someone else's plight through our own experience and to share our situation with him or her through stories and anecdotes. There is nothing wrong with that. However, most of the sufferings of Christ were different from ours. The reality was that His physical, emotional, and spiritual sufferings far outweighed any suffering you or I will ever go through. Christ knows exactly what your trial is like. He understands exactly what it means to be human, with every facet and every complication. The reality of His suffering, however, is that it was all for you. He suffered for your sake. Each lash of the whip against His back, punch to His face, kick to His side, nail piercing, and pained breath on the cross was so that He might know you, and you might know Him.

Why does Peter say to rejoice in Christ's sufferings? Doesn't that seem strange and out of place, like an oxymoron? How can we rejoice when life hurts or doesn't make sense? Peter is saying that what Christ's suffering bought is worth rejoicing in. His suffering brought your salvation. The worst tragedy in human history, Christ's execution, brought about God's greatest triumph—your salvation and reconciliation to the Lord. Isn't that worth rejoicing in?

Your suffering will have good in it, though it is so hard to see that right now. You will see yourself and others grow more like Christ. You will see the goodness of the Lord in your misery and despair, and you can rejoice knowing He is with you, present at every moment of your life. Christ's suffering was temporary, and yours is temporary too. Yet both will have eternal glory. Our lives are short, a mere vapor and mist, quickly present and quickly gone. The greater glory comes *after* the suffering—the glory of Christ.

NO ADVERSITY, NO WISDOM

"It is better to go to the house of mourning than to go to the house of feasting, for this is the end of all mankind, and the living will lay it to heart. Sorrow is better than laughter, for by sadness of face the heart is made glad. The heart of the wise is in the house of mourning, but the heart of fools is in the house of mirth. It is better for a man to hear the rebuke of the wise than to hear the song of fools. For as the crackling of thorns under a pot, so is the laughter of the fools; this also is vanity" ~Ecclesiastes 7:2–6

King Solomon had everything a person could ever want and was the envy of everyone in Israel—and the world—during his reign. There was nothing he desired that he couldn't have; the world was literally at his fingertips. Yet Ecclesiastes is the book that brings perspective to life— to the rich, to the poor, to the strong, and to the weak. Solomon had been given wisdom, the greatest gift aside from salvation. It's a sobering read about our lives in this world. It also serves as an exhortation to live our lives focused on Christ and not on the things of this world.

Solomon, even at the end of his life, was not one to sit around in self-pity. He was not king of the pity party, but he understood that growth in the Lord didn't happen in the perfect life. It happened in the deep, dark shadows of the valley, where partying and mirth were not present. If we're honest with ourselves, we seek pleasure, prosperity, and comfort in this life. Sadly, we cannot grow the most in the Lord while in the lap of luxury, comfort, and fun. We need to embrace the trials of this life for the sake of growing closer to the Lord.

Most Christians today would flee from trials like running from a lion, a foe, or an enemy. We say we want to grown in wisdom and grace, the reality is, we desire the ease and comfort of the world while growing in wisdom and grace. As a Christ-follower, we cannot have it both ways. John MacArthur says in his Bible notes for the above passage, "to emphasize that more is learned from adversity from pleasure. True wisdom is developed in the crucible of life's trials." I pray you will see the Lord's wisdom in your life over this world and choose the road that will provide true wisdom, God's wisdom.

UNIQUE STRUGGLES

"Your eyes saw my unformed substance; in your book were written, every one of them,
the days that were formed for me,
when as yet there was none of them" ~Psalm 139:16

We like to compare ourselves with others. It is the envy of the Joneses next door—we're trying to keep up with them and make sure that our grass is as green as theirs, if not greener. Social media doesn't help our envy, jealousy, and comparisons either. Even in the misery of our trials we like to compare. Theodore Roosevelt wisely said, "Comparison is the thief of joy."

In both good and bad times, we compare. It is human nature, but rarely does it do us any good. Your trial is yours, just as your calling is yours. No person on this earth was called to endure what you are enduring or to live the life God has assigned to you. There may be similarities, but God has specifically and uniquely called you to your life, to your journey, to your struggle. Think about Psalm 139. God has written each of your days before you even lived one of them.

While it's good to talk with others who are in the same situation or who have gone before you, don't try to compare your stories. It's easy to think, "They had it much easier than I do," or even the opposite. No two trials are the same, so walk your journey with the grace the Lord has bestowed upon you. The reality is that God is working in your life and in someone else's life. Seeing God work in and through your life, knowing your eternal future, makes it all worth while.

God is the author of your story. Everything in your life was ordained for you, by His hands, for His sovereign plan for the world. No one else but you can play your part, and you can't play anyone else's part.

MOUNTAINS WILL MOVE

"Truly I say to you, if you have faith like a grain of mustard seed, you will say to this mountain, 'Move from here to there,' and it will move, and nothing will be impossible for you" ~Matthew 17:20

Jesus had quite a time with his disciples. They didn't always understand his parables and were simple-minded, just like we probably are. In trying to help them understand faith, Jesus told them about the mustard seed, a miniscule seed. Jesus said that even if your faith in Him is as small as a mustard seed, you will do amazing things—like moving mountains. He might mean actual mountains, but He more likely means that you will be able to do great things in accomplishing His will. Mountains are nearly impossible for a human to move, but that's the point Jesus is making. With faith in Christ, even faith as small as a mustard seed, you will be able to do the impossible. It's not you doing the impossible; it is Christ.

Your trial is currently a mountain for you. It's difficult to move; it's stubborn. There's a hard road ahead of you, with a difficult climb. And yet, as a Christ-follower, you are to have the faith that Jesus is talking about in this passage. You can only move mountains by surrendering yourself before God in dependence on Him. You may not have the faith of a warrior, but that's not what Jesus is seeking. He's looking for faith the size of a seed. In Christ you will have victory; you will be able to do that which seems absolutely impossible. Through Christ's power in your life, mountains will move; you will change; and the world will change.

As Luke writes, foretelling the birth of Christ in Luke 1:37, "For nothing will be impossible with God." I pray that you will see God at work in the seemingly impossible circumstances you are presently going through, knowing and trusting that He can move mountains. All Christ is asking for is faith the size of a mustard seed. According to Christ, that is great faith.

121

ENTRUST YOUR SOUL

"Therefore, let those who suffer according to God's will entrust their souls to a faithful Creator while doing good" ~1 Peter 4:19

As a Christ-follower you have already given your soul, your life, and prayerfully, your everything to Christ. You have hopefully laid at His feet your dreams, hopes, aspirations, and desires. The question now becomes: Will you surrender your trial to Him?

In any trial it's hard to get a sense of peace about what's happening; it's hard to have peace, and it's hard to hand over your plight to God. Trials aren't meant for peace, that doesn't mean we can't have peace in them. Each day and each night you may have to pray the Lord's will over each moment. You may have to pray it continually, which is even more difficult in these dark times. Giving up your entire life to the Lord is difficult. You want to be in charge; you want control; you want to direct your future. You have expectations and things you want to do. Yet God has different plans; and a trial is a way for Him to redirect your path into your great good and His greater glory. Lay everything at His feet and entrust your soul to Him.

Peter knew this and had seen it. That is why he encouraged us to entrust all that we are and all that we have to One who was faithful, is faithful, and will be faithful into eternity. He saw Christ's promises come true, not just for himself, but for the church. In writing this, Peter wants you to know that as you lay your will at Christ's feet, there will be peace and comfort for you in any situation. The Spirit is going to work in your life through prayer and the Word to gift you in this peace.

Peter was not giving us an option, rather a command. At some point you will entrust your trial to Christ. Find peace, my brothers and sisters, in the Lord.

SUFFICIENT FOR THE DAY
(OR EVEN THE HOUR)

"Is not life more than food,
and the body more than clothing?" ~Matthew 6:25

Most likely you and I have had to learn to live day by day—to take life one day at a time. I had to learn to do this from the day I found out about the brain tumor and the subsequent diagnosis of cancer until the crisis subsided. Now I have learned to live my life this way. The reality for several months was that I needed to take life one hour at a time, sometimes even a half hour at a time. You probably know exactly how that feels.

It's hard not to worry. Am I going to have enough money for food and housing? Is this MRI going to come back clear? Did that job interview go well? Will the doctor have any answers? Will my significant other stay so we can work things out? Worrying is a human condition, one we all share, even if we like to think the opposite. Worry shows our frailty and yet allows God's sovereignty in our lives. Jesus knew the frailties of life for humans. He knew we would worry about tomorrow. He even knew we would worry hour to hour, minute to minute.

Matthew 6 is His answer to our worries, whether we have petty worries, like what we'll wear, or significant worries, like, "Will I survive this?" In this chapter, Jesus talks about caring and providing for the sparrows—such insignificant creatures compared to people. Yet Christ cares and provides for them, not just as a group of birds, but also as individual sparrows. The reality of sparrows is that they worry about absolutely nothing. They know God is going to provide for their every need. This should bring comfort to your soul. Christ cares more abundantly for you than all the sparrows on the earth.

Verse 33 is His command to you in this trial: "Seek first the kingdom of God and His righteousness, and all these things will be added to you."

His answer to worrying is to seek first the kingdom, not your needs. In the end you will be taken care of by a great and loving Savior who knows all the needs of your heart and your life. Seek first His kingdom, Christian!

FOR GREATER PURPOSE

"As for you, you meant evil against me,
but God meant it for good" ~Genesis 50:20

We often run away from trials and hardships in this life (especially in the United States); it's a natural reaction. We literally do not want them and willingly curse and reject these precious gifts from God. We fail to see them as a challenge to overcome, an opportunity to grow. It is natural to not like pain and suffering. It is human to run from that which hurts and stings. However, as Christ-followers it's strategic that we see the work of the Lord in every area of our lives, both the good and the bad. Each has its place in growing us to be more like His Son. Running away from hard times is running away from God.

The reality of trials is that God has greater plans for us both during and after the trial than we could ever imagine. God's calling in this trial has many facets. One facet is that God is planning to use us greatly at some point during, or after, the trial. Those who want to be used by the Lord are willing to be tested. Those who want to do great things for God will embrace the trials the Lord allows, because it prepares them, in Him, to be used for whatever purpose and to whatever end His will determines in this life. God can't use those who are stuck in the façade of a perfect life. Green grass; large bank accounts; pretty-pictured, photoshopped families—they're all great, but God can't use those who are like everybody else or pretending to be like everybody else. He has to do His work in us to break us of our lives, to give us new perspectives, to give us a specific calling beyond the easy life everyone else is living.

Take a look at Moses. He was raised in a palace, had to endure the trial of understanding his past, spent forty years in the wilderness to then return and endure the Lord's calling to bring the Jews out of Egypt, then endured another forty years of their whining and complaining in the wilderness. Yet Moses pressed on toward the purposes the Lord laid on him. The entire goal was to bring the people of the Lord to the borders of the Promised Land.

Or look at Joseph, who came hundreds of years before Moses. He was the favored child of his father, Jacob. He had everything he could ever want. Yet God had a different plan. His brothers despised him. They meant to kill him, but decided to sell him into slavery instead, where he was then sold to an Egyptian official, falsely accused of adultery, imprisoned for several years, and finally raised to the second highest position in all of Egypt. Only the pharaoh had more power. For what purpose was this done? The purpose was to save a small group of Abraham's descendants, who would one day become a mighty people. As Joseph says, "As for you, you meant evil against me, but God meant it for good."

In the darkness of prison, Joseph didn't see the end. He didn't know why he was there. Moses, in his first time in the desert, didn't know why he was taken away from the luxuries of Egypt into utter poverty and desolation. It is the same for you. You don't know God's end goal in your life, but like Joseph and Moses you are called to trust and to go where the Lord is leading you. You may not be suffering to save a group of people, but what if you were put in this trial so that one person would be brought to Christ in salvation? Would that make it all worth it? I hope that one day you will exclaim, "Absolutely!" Or what if it were to encourage and raise the spirits of someone else who was suffering? In the end God is going to use you greatly. He's tested you for a purpose, and His testing is not a waste in any way. He has great purpose for you—just believe!

A.W. Tozer says, "God never uses anyone greatly until He tests them deeply." God is going to use you greatly!

THE GREATEST LIFE

"But whatever gain I had, I counted as loss for the sake of Christ. Indeed, I count everything as loss because of the surpassing worth of knowing Christ Jesus my Lord. For his sake I have suffered the loss of all things and count them as rubbish, in order that I may gain Christ" ~Philippians 3:7–8

God has given you a great gift in calling you to tribulation. It sounds strange, but He wants to walk with you through this season, and it is His joy to take your hand and lead you down some very treacherous paths. He delights that you are depending upon Him, that your faith and trust in Him is growing, and that you are doing so in Him with each breath. The journey isn't delightful, but being in the company of Jesus on this journey is.

My pastor, Todd Smith, said in a sermon just before my first surgery, "The Christian life isn't the easiest life; it's the greatest life." Jesus never promised ease and comfort in this life. He never said that anywhere in the Bible, and don't believe anyone who tells you it's there. But following the greatest man to ever live, die, and live again is the greatest thing you could ever do, and you are doing that right now.

I'm sure you've heard the saying, "Your best life now." Is that true for you right now? Is it really your best life, hooked up to machines in the ICU? Is it your best life in the unemployment line? Is it really your best life if you've been abandoned and are now all alone? Is your best life found in persecution? Jesus said that we would suffer as His followers. He also said that the best was yet to come.

Your best life is always ahead of you, never behind you or in the past, because, as a Christ-follower, heaven is your future. The reality is that in this world your best life is always yet to be. Maybe the saying should read, "Your best faith now."

THE HUMANITY OF CHRIST

"And he said, 'Abba, Father, all things are possible for you. Remove this cup from me. Yet not what I will, but what you will'" ~Mark 14:36

Take a moment and read through this passage of Christ in the Garden of Gethsemane in Mark 14. He is hours away from His crucifixion, impending death, and final resurrection.

Jesus is 100 percent God and 100 percent man. It's good to focus on His deity, but there is a surprising truth about His humanity. In His humanity He was just like us: He got hungry and tired; He smiled and laughed. In His suffering He acted just as you are probably acting in your trial: with trepidation, but with dependence on God.

His time in the Garden of Gethsemane was His worst trial up to that point. Christ was walking ahead, in time, toward His crucifixion. It is in this intimate prayer with the Father that we see Christ's humanity most clearly. He demonstrates His humanity more in Mark 14 than anywhere else in scripture. His prayer sounds so very much like ours would in the same situation. After the Last Supper and time with the disciples, Jesus left the city of Jerusalem to walk a short distance to the garden. He left His disciples to go pray to the Father regarding His upcoming execution.

The first thing we see of His humanity is in verse 34: "My soul is very sorrowful, even to death." Have you ever felt that—that your soul was so troubled that you might not survive? It could be the loss of a loved one, a friend, job, health, or comfort. It's the thought: "What do I do now?" It's that heavy burden that He bore in the garden, and it's a heavy burden you bear. The weight of your trial seems insurmountable, and it seems that the only way out of it is through dying.

The second thing is Christ's physical exhaustion. After Jesus left His beloved disciples in one part of the garden, He went a little farther and collapsed. The physical exhaustion of the past week and the physical effects of the torment of His soul weighed so heavily upon Him that He stumbled and collapsed. If Jesus had been calm during this time, Mark would not have said that He "fell on the ground." He would have said that Jesus kneeled, sat down, or rested before praying. But He fell on the ground and poured out His heart to the Lord. The heaviness of what was to come weighed down upon His body and soul.

We see Christ's transparency in verse 36 when He prayed, "Abba, Father, all things are possible for You. Remove this cup from Me. Yet not what I will, but what You will." Wow, there is so much there for us in our trial just in this short prayer. This was Jesus's first prayer during His time in the garden. It is incredible to read His anguish and how He poured Himself out to the Lord.

Christ first acknowledged His place before His Father. Christ who helped develop the plan of His own crucifixion acknowledged that at this point the Father was in complete control of the situation. Jesus declared that all things were possible. God knew that in order to bring about salvation, Jesus had to be crucified. Jesus embraced the trial.

The next part of His prayer shows the depths of His humanity. Jesus prayed for God to remove the crucifixion. It's not that Christ didn't want to do whatever was necessary to save humanity. He just wished there were another way—another way that wasn't as excruciatingly painful and humiliating.

As Jesus ended this first part of His garden prayer, He said, "Yet not what I will, but what You will." While he declared in the previous part of the prayer that He would like to find another way, He gave up His own will. The plan that He, the Father, and the Spirit created for the salvation of mankind before time began was the plan that Jesus was going to fulfill. All of history was culminating in what Jesus was about to endure. As Jesus's suffering was about to begin, He was willing to move ahead, knowing the will of the Lord. In your own suffering, are you willing to look at the example of Christ and move ahead? Jesus embraced the will of God, as difficult as it was. Will you?

COMFORT OF CHRIST

"Now may our Lord Jesus Christ himself, and God our Father,
who loved us and gave us eternal comfort and good hope
through grace, comfort your hearts and establish them
in every good work and word" ~2 Thessalonians 2:16–17

In many of the Apostle Paul's letters he stops a moment to pray for those who are reading the letter. While he is writing to a specific group of believers, living in a certain time and place, Paul prays this for all believers who will come in the future. In these short, beautiful prayers we see a man of God praying for people he will never meet this side of heaven.

He reminds us of Christ and what Christ's presence through His Spirit in our lives brings. Notice that Christ's small blessings are not tied to our situation, but are always there, as Christ is always there in our lives. His presence is the blessing. We will face some dark, uncertain days ahead—if not now, then someday. Paul writes a few things to bring us peace, including eternal comfort, hope through grace, comfort of heart, and good works. Notice that Paul says, "eternal comfort." We are exhorted not to get too comfortable in this world; our comfort is yet to come with Him in eternity in heaven. Hope is only to be found in Christ. The hope of God is everlasting and will not fail. Our hope in the things of this world, or in relationships, or in possessions fails. Our hope must be in Christ through the grace that He has bestowed on us as His children. In Christ's presence we find comforts that will take away all anxieties of life. Lastly, while trials are many times full of negative situations, they can and will eventually result in good works. Think of the people who are encouraged by the work God is doing in our lives or of those who see our faith and decide to follow Christ in faith. Think of all the good that will come from our trials—more good than we will ever know in this life.

Only good can come from God working in your life.

TAKE HOLD

"Fight the good fight of faith. Take hold of the eternal life to which you were called and about which you made the good confession in the presence of many witnesses" ~1 Timothy 6:12

We were never meant to live in the world like it is, corrupted as it is by our sin. This world is not our home, and there are some trials of this life where we are confronted with a very stark reality—our mortality, another part of being human that wasn't supposed to happen. For me, brain cancer has some very bleak prospects, and while I cherish each day, my trial gave me a unique and rare opportunity to consider my own mortality. Contemplating our mortality is one of the greatest things we as Christ-followers can do. It gives us an incredible perspective on this life and helps us truly live a life in which we pursue Christ with each blessed day.

In so many ways you have to "take hold of eternal life." You have to fight in this life for the next life. Knowing that someday your presence in this world will end should give you great strength, purpose, and perspective. Your trial will have a way of reorienting your life to what really matters—Christ, and living each moment of this life for Him.

Your trial, your fight, is a good fight. It is a fight for your faith, but as Paul writes, it's a "good fight." Fight on, my friends. With God on your side, only good can come in this struggle.

THE LIVING DYING

*"But if Christ is in you, although the body is dead because of sin,
the Spirit is life because of righteousness. If the Spirit of him who raised Jesus from
the dead dwells in you, he who raised Christ Jesus
from the dead will also give life to your mortal bodies
through his Spirit who dwells in you"* ~Romans 8:10–11

I can bet that at some point in this journey you've gotten tired, if not flat out exhausted and fatigued beyond what you've ever experienced in life. Our bodies have limits, and many times the physical, emotional, and spiritual strain of the troubles we face in this life take a greater toll on our bodies than our best workout at the gym. You and I can't live like we did when we were teenagers in high school, thinking that we are invincible and immortal. Our lives are short on this earth, and our bodies are dying because of our sin. In God's design for creation, we were never meant to die, but we do, as a consequence of our sin—yours, mine, all of ours, throughout all of history. We live in a world where everyone dies. It truly is a life of death in this world. Even more than physical death, we live in a world where the majority of people are dying spiritually.

The reality though for the Christ-follower is that while we are dying physically, we are also living spiritually. Christ is life, and as His Spirit dwells within you, you have life in Him. You will die someday, but afterward you will live forever in the life of Christ. Most of the world cannot say that. Our trials are an opportunity for us to engage unbelievers in our mortality and to point them toward the hope of life in Christ.

I pray you will take hold of this truth: you, the physical you, will fall and fail. Your bones and muscles will weaken, but you will thrive so greatly spiritually. Realize, Christ-follower, that Paul is writing an incredible truth in saying that the Spirit who raised Christ from the dead also dwells in you. It's not that the Spirit comes and goes as He pleases; He is committed to you. His dwelling place is your soul (Ephesians 1:13). Think about it, Christ raised Himself from the dead—nothing and no one else did. It was He who conquered sin and death. This same Spirit resides in you and in your trial to exhibit to a dying world the Lord's presence and grace in your life. Whatever you face in your struggles, the truth is that it cannot overtake you, because the Spirit is yours, and He will work in your life from the inside out. While He is the keeper of your body, He is also more greatly the keeper of your soul. In Christ, your soul is secure.

WE'RE ALL HAVING SURGERY

"And I will give you a new heart, and a new spirit I will put within you. And I will remove the heart of stone from your flesh and give you a heart of flesh" ~Ezekiel 36:26

Mike Gaston, one of my former pastors and a great friend, wrote the following post about cancer—of the body and of the soul—on his weekly blog, *Sabbath Thoughts.*

Cancer of the soul is far worse and more serious than that of the body. Mike writes:

> As I walked away from my friend Adam's hospital room, I was struck by what he was about to do. In a couple of hours, he was going to voluntarily allow someone to put him to sleep so another man could cut open his skull and take something out of his brain that didn't belong there.
>
> Wow. Think about that for a minute. How do you DO that? We had gotten together a few days earlier to talk about his upcoming cancer surgery. He said that it was good to be with someone who knew what cancer was about, and it's true that my own recent experience with breast cancer had created a bond between us.
>
> I was glad that I could encourage him, but to be honest, losing my left breast sounded very different to me than brain surgery.
>
> What does it take to submit to that kind of an operation? What core convictions were necessary to keep Adam from running out of the hospital and getting as far away from a scalpel as possible? I think there are two:
>
> "I will be much better off when this procedure is done."

Adam knew that he could not ignore the news that there was a malignant lump in his brain—the consequences would be lethal. He also knew that, whatever pain would come as a result of the surgery, it was necessary for his long-term health.

"I trust the people who are operating on me." Adam was literally placing his life in the hands of his doctors, confident that their skill would allow him to wake up to a better life. In this case, happily, they did their work well. He came home a few days after the procedure, and was there to welcome his students to his classroom when school started in [the fall of 2014].

On a recent Sabbath hike, I realized that God calls us all to a similar mind-set. As the Great Physician, He is constantly operating on us—in fact, long before such surgeries existed, He told His people that they needed heart transplants (Ezekiel 36:26). He is shaping us, changing us, removing that which harms us and keeps us from pleasing Him.

Those same two convictions are necessary to this process:

"I will be much better off when His work is done." I want what He wants for me—to be like Christ. So I welcome His examination, and I willingly submit to His surgery, even when it hurts. I know that in the long run, I will be glad for it.

"I trust the One who is operating on me." I know that He works for my good and for His glory. He knows what He is doing, even when I don't. Especially when I don't.

Those convictions allowed me to pray this prayer on that hike – I invite you to pray it with me:

"Lord, there is in me that which doesn't belong. I admit that I don't hate it as much as I should — some of it I cling to, although it is bad for me and dishonors you. I trust You, and know that I will be better off when You change me. So even if it hurts, change me."

The cancer needs to go. That process can be painful. But as any cancer survivor could tell you, it's worth it.

* * *

https://sabbaththoughts.wordpress.com/2014/08/15/were-all-having-surgery/

YET TO SEE

"But God chose what is foolish in the world to shame the wise;
God chose what is weak in the world to shame the strong;
God chose what is low and despised in the world, even things that are not, to bring to
nothing things that are, so that no human being
might boast in the presence of God" ~1 Corinthians 1:27–29

As a history buff—and a buff history teacher, no less!—I love that there are many people we study in my class who have had a great impact in our world's past. Many of the people we study are corrupt, self-absorbed, care nothing for the people who are socially "underneath" them, and believe that history will put them in the best light, despite their poor character, conduct, and failings. Great people never declare themselves as such. Most of the great people in this world will never make the history books; they're too busy changing people's lives. The reality is that few people we study in history are good people, and there are even fewer who are great people. Our world lacks great people, even in the good times, but especially in the bad times.

Christ-follower, God brought you into this trial to make you a great person—not according to the ways many people think, but in line with His ways. In your trial He is molding and shaping you into His likeness so that through Christ you may be a great person, working toward His plan of accomplishing His will for His great purpose and greater glory.

Though great people rarely make the history books, take a look at the church. The chairs are filled with amazing people, many of whom have tread some extremely difficult valleys in life and who have come to see that because of the great work of God in our lives and by the presence of Christ, we are great people.

Great people aren't made from a carefree life on the beach. They are made from the harshest storms, in the deepest waters of this life.

The reality is that great people *do* make history, but the history they make is rarely in books; it's seen in changed lives. Great people pour themselves out for the work of Christ and into the lives of people they meet—and even into those they may never meet, those who are observing from a distance. Each person they meet and converse with takes something away. Thus, at the end of their days, they don't see their life as one for the history books but they see its impact in the changed lives that continue to flourish long after they have passed. They have literally poured so much into others that there is nothing left for the history books; they have given themselves away.

God is looking for people to trust in Him—people He can use to change lives and grow His kingdom. In your trial He is choosing you for this great calling. On your own, by yourself, you are not a great person, but with Christ by your side—with His name written upon your soul— you will be great. History may not remember you, but the people you encounter will recall the work of Christ in your life and how you entrusted your soul and livelihood to Him.

Minister Henry Varley says, "The world has yet to see what God will do with and for and through and in and by the man who is fully consecrated to Him."

Are you in? Are you willing to pour yourself and your journey with Jesus into the lives of this world? Are you willing to live a great life, not for history, but for saved souls?

TWO SPARROWS

"Are not two sparrows sold for a penny? And not one of them will fall to the ground apart from your Father. But even the hairs of your head are all numbered" ~Matthew 10:29–30

Jesus is the great comforter, and here He is trying to calm His followers regarding the anxieties of this life. In His power, God is taking care of you, but in His greater power He is even caring for each sparrow, a tiny bird completely insignificant in the scheme of this life. To reiterate the Lord's care for you, Jesus refers to something even more insignificant than mere birds—the hairs on your head.

We think the hair on our head is quite important. We fuss over it each day, cut it every so often, worry about its color, or even fret over the number of hairs left on our head. Jesus says there is nothing that happens without His knowing or allowing it to happen. He knows each hair that turns gray and each hair that falls out. He knows it all.

With sparrows and hair, Jesus is illustrating how important you are to Him. If He knows and cares about these two small details of our world, just think about how much He cares for you, His magnificent creation. He knows about each job interview, each doctor's appointment, each stab of the needle, each conversation with friends, each sigh of the heart, and each prayer. Do not ever think that you are insignificant to God in your trial. Christ hears every heartbeat and every heart's cry, and it is He who will act, in His time, to make you more Christlike. He wants His best for you.

For me, God infinitely knew each cancer cell that was growing in my brain. He is also intimately familiar with your plight—every second of it. There is nothing He misses in your life. If He cares so deeply for something like a bird, will not God care so very greatly for you, His dearly beloved child? He will not let you fall from His hand.

I leave you with this truth, "Who shall separate us from the love of Christ? Shall tribulation, or distress, or persecution, or famine, or nakedness, or danger, or sword?... No, in all these things we are more than conquerors through him who loved us. For I am sure that neither death nor life…will be able to separate us from the love of God in Christ Jesus our Lord." (*Romans 8:35–39*)

Truly the answer is that no one and nothing can separate us from Him, His love, and His great purpose for those who call Him Lord.

GOOD AFFLICTION?

"It is good for me that I was afflicted, that I might learn your statutes ... your hands have made and fashioned me; give me understanding that I may learn your commandments" ~Psalm 119:71, 73

Psalm 119 is an amazing psalm. It is the longest of the psalms and the longest chapter in the Bible. However, two verses stick out in our time of suffering. We don't know the exact affliction of the psalmist, but, as in our lives, it is a God-directed trial. We do know the psalmist says his affliction is good, and my prayer for you is that someday you will say the same of your own affliction. He writes about God's purpose in affliction—that we might learn His statutes or His ways. We have looked at how God is showing Himself in your trial; He is drawing you to Him through His Word.

In his affliction the psalmist prayed for understanding, but it's very different from the understanding we pray for. We pray to understand our situation; we want to know the reasons why we are enduring such hardship. I'm sure the psalmist had those same prayers for understanding, but he learned a new perspective on his troubles. He prayed for understanding so he could know God better. He saw the connection between affliction and growth in the Lord, and he relished it. Throughout Psalm 119 we see the passion of the psalmist for God's Word, because it's how he got to know God. He wanted to know God better than he did, and he knew his plight was an opportunity to do so. That's more purposeful to the author than understanding all the complexities of his own situation. Knowing the Lord became his life's pursuit, beyond the pain of his struggles.

The goodness the psalmist talks about is knowing God. It's almost as if his trial is nothing compared to knowing the Lord, and he is correct. Knowing God far outweighs any troubles we may face. I pray that you will find this to be true for yourself. Take this time of suffering to know the One who will show Himself faithful to you.

ALL JOY

"Count it all joy, my brothers, when you meet trials of various kinds, for you know that the testing of your faith produces steadfastness. And let steadfastness have its full effect, that you may be perfect and complete. Lacking in nothing" ~James 1:2–4

Of all New Testament writers, James most likely knew Jesus the best. He was Jesus's half-brother and wasn't always keen about what Jesus came to do. He did not become a follower of Christ until sometime after Jesus's resurrection and probably even after His ascension into heaven. Nonetheless, he was a witness to the extraordinary life, death, and resurrection of Jesus and could attest to the trials Jesus faced, as well as the ones he faced as a Christ-follower.

Trials and hardships were on the mind of James as he wrote. He opened the book by discussing trials, and he knew that bringing encouragement during trials was of utmost importance to his readers. It's almost like he started the book: "Hi, this is James, let's talk about your struggles in life and why you have them." There was no flowery introduction to his book. He got right to the point.

Let me ask you something. Do you have joy—not happiness, but joy—in your present circumstances? Happiness is fleeting and based on feelings, which for most of us are here one minute and gone the next. Feelings are also great at betraying us. No doubt, you may not have the most positive feelings right now. Joy, though, is not based on feelings but is about God. Can you consider your life a joy because God is in control? Can you consider that you are saved and secure in the salvation bought by Jesus? That's where joy is found—not in our passing circumstances but in our relationship with Christ. You can be joyful without happiness. Joy is a deep and abiding peace and comfort in the work of the Lord, while happiness is tied to our experiences—the ups and the downs of our lives. No one is going to be happy in the hospital, in broken relationships, in the unemployment line, in the midst of hurt feelings, but a Christ-follower can demonstrate great joy because his or her situation is not secured to this world but to God, who is not confined to this world or the troubles of this world. On the cross, Christ conquered the troubles of this world for your good, your joy, and His glory.

Happiness is fleeting, joy is abiding. May joy abide in and through you both in the easy and hard times of your life.

I WILL RAISE UP...

"In that day I will raise up the booth of David that is fallen
and repair its breaches, and raise up its ruins,
and rebuild it as in the days of old" ~Amos 9:11

David's life was nothing but miraculous. As a shepherd boy he was
chosen king of Israel, the one to replace King Saul. As a young shepherd
boy, he defeated the massive Goliath. He became a mighty warrior, a
man after God's own heart, and eventually king over all of Israel.
Consider for a moment that David was one of those people where all of
life seemed to work out. He was seemingly the person that couldn't
seem to fail at anything. With God, David couldn't fail, even though
King Saul sought David's demise. With God you cannot fail, because
God is not a god of failure. Everything He does ends in success.

The reality for David at the end of his life was that he messed up: he
sinned with Bathsheba and murdered Uriah, Bathsheba's husband. You
could say David failed miserably. David was falling apart at the end of
his life. His son, Absalom, challenged David for the throne; his family
was broken apart; and the future of the Davidic kingdom was in
question, even though God had promised the Messiah would come
from the line of David. Just a few generations later the kingdom would
split and later be taken into captivity. David as a human failed, just as we
fail. Only in Christ can we ultimately succeed.

Yet here's God's word through the prophet Amos: "In that day, I
will raise up the booths of David that is fallen and repair its breaches,
and raise up its ruins, and rebuild it as in the days of old." The Lord will
raise us up from our failures and sins. As a Christ-follower, you have
been raised up through salvation.

God was making a promise to David, and in a way, He is making
that same promise to you. God made a promise in Romans 8:28 that
says, "And we know that for those who love God all things work
together for good, for those who are called according to his purpose."
Paul was saying something here that was similar to that of Amos. David

144

was called by God, just like we as Christ-followers are. Amos was writing long after David, but God kept His promise to restore and repair to David that which was broken in his life.

The same is going to happen to you sometime after this trial. The Lord is going to restore and repair that which was broken. But take notice: this doesn't happen for David until long after David had passed from this earth. David had been dead and buried for quite some time when God told us through Amos that He was going to restore and repair the line of David in the promised Messiah, Jesus Christ. We don't know how God is going to do this in our lives, and the reality we need to understand is that these things may not happen in our lifetime. But they will happen. Christ-followers, those who belong to Christ, will go to heaven and start living life as God intended it to be. Life will only get better with Christ, even in the storm.

God will raise up the ruins and rebuild our lives in Christ.

WHEN THE ROAD DARKENS

*"A friend loves at all times, and a brother is born
for adversity" ~Proverbs 17:17*

One of the amazing gifts in our trials is the number of people who walk
with us through them. I was so very blessed by an incredible group of
Christ-followers and also unbelievers who said they would walk with me
into the valley—into the dark—and would stay with me until whatever
end the Lord willed. I pray that you find a faithful group beside you to
walk this trial with. If not, please rest assured that I'm praying for you
and walking this road with you through prayer. I'm rooting for your
victory in Christ. So at least one person is already by your side, and it is
my great joy to be that person.

There were some who started the journey and didn't walk through
its entirety, some who came midway through, and others who were
curiously absent from the whole journey. In my journey some were new
friends, some were renewed or strengthened friendships, and sadly,
some friendships diminished.

J.R.R. Tolkien profoundly wrote: "Faithless is he who says farewell
when the road darkens." Many times during a trial you will see who your
true friends are. You will also see who the fair-weather friends are, those
who hang around while the weather is good and the times are carefree,
fun, and easy, but when things go bad and get difficult, they flee. It's
hard to question an individual's choices and motives, but the reality is
that many who leave when darkness arrives appear to be faithless. They
don't see Christ in your struggles; they don't want to deal with whatever
pain and heartache you may encounter; they don't see that your journey
is also their own.

Many fade from your life because they possibly don't want to face a
trial in their own life, or they just don't know what to say, so they
possibly say nothing, leading to a fractured friendship.

Then there are those who stay for a season and move on when that season is over, and that is normal.

Aside from the trial, this may be one of the hardest things you'll go through. People you thought would be there are no longer. The reality is that you expected them to walk with you because you would have done the same for them, or you at least thought that they would be there, no matter what. Don't be too harsh with them though. You may have to separate yourself from their friendship for a while—which they've already done with you—but know that God has something for them in this trial as well. Remember that this is a journey for so many, including those who don't walk with you. Like a rock thrown in a lake, you may not ever know how the ripples of your impact will touch people.

Someday you may have the opportunity to discuss your journey with those individuals—what you learned and all that Christ did in and through you. Have love, grace, and purpose in your discussion with them; hope and pray that they are willing to listen and learn, because the end goal for all is to grow closer to the Lord.

As you pray for your own journey along the way, pray for theirs and for all who are with you through the days ahead. One of the hardest parts for those who chose not to walk with you will be that you have learned so much and grown so much. Those who weren't with you missed out on the great joys and sorrows of the trial in your life; they missed out on growing closer to you and the Lord; they missed seeing Christ in your life and also their life. All is not over for them though. As long as Christ's light shines there is always hope.

"Faithless is he" who doesn't walk with you, but faithful is He who does.

STRENGTHENED IN CHRIST

"I can do all things through him who strengthens me" ~*Philippians 4:13*

No doubt you've heard this verse many times on your journey. It is a well-known verse, but is there something in it that could give insight on what it really means, and on how you can be encouraged in Christ? Do you ever look at this verse as one of those mountaintop verses, like, "I've conquered Mount Everest and praise God for His strength?"

What you need right now is strength—maybe physical strength, but more importantly, you need spiritual strength. In calling you to this trial, Jesus is taking you places you never imagined, and as such, you will need a strength beyond this world, because this trial is from beyond this world, and your strength in this world will not suffice. This isn't one of those verses where you can literally do anything you desire, such as swim the English Channel, be an Olympic champion, or be in the *Guinness Book of Records*. This verse cannot be taken so flippantly and ignorantly. No, what Paul is saying is that in Christ you can do anything the Lord has planned for you—not in your strength, but in the strength given by Christ to accomplish His will. In Christ, you can do all things for His kingdom.

Paul saw the strength of Christ as he endured beatings, shipwrecks, court trials, prison cells, and persecution, all in the name of Christ. It was Christ who gave him the strength to encourage churches through his letters, and to continue preaching the gospel wherever he went. He couldn't do it alone, nor could he do it in his own strength. To accomplish out-of-this-world tasks, you need an out-of-this-world strength—Christ's strength through His presence.

The focus of this passage is on Christ, not you. The story of our lives is not about us, but about Christ, and in Him we get the opportunity to be a part of accomplishing His will.

UNPLANNED

"From of old no one has heard or perceived by the ear, no eye has seen a God besides you, who acts for those who wait for him" ~Isaiah 64:4

You had expectations for your life, just like every other person whose life was supposed to be so very different. You weren't supposed to be in the place you are currently in right now. Remember, though, that you are a part of a greater story, God's story. As John Piper wrote in a *Solid Joys* entry: "Your agonizing, unplanned detour is not a waste—not if you look to the Lord for His unexpected work, and do what you must do in His name." (*Colossians 3:17*) "The Lord works for those who wait for Him." (*Isaiah 64:4*) You play the part for which He has assigned you. For the few of us who are blessed with suffering, we get to see God work a detour into our lives toward a greater existence and a brighter future that is directed and guided by His beautiful, sovereign hand.

As I recovered from my surgeries, radiation, and chemo, I began to put life together again, to see what was left, and to see where life was going—i.e., to rebuild. I realized that my life had completely changed, and I could not return to the way it was before, nor would I choose for that to happen. It felt as if the careless and carefree life was gone, and the reality was that it *was* gone. And yet my life is now filled with a deeper purpose, wider perspective, and greater appreciation of life. It is a new life, and in so many ways a better life.

Jesus doesn't waste anything. His work is always fruitful, and though it's hard to see, our walk through this valley will also be fruitful. It is never a waste. We may discard our suffering, but Jesus won't. Don't waste your suffering.

* * *

http://solidjoys.desiringgod.org/en/devotionals/
god-s-design-in-detours

SUFFER TOGETHER, REJOICE TOGETHER

"That the members may have the same care for one another.
If one member suffers all suffer, together; if one member is honored, all rejoice together.
Now you are the body of Christ
and individually members of it" ~1 Corinthians 12:25–27

One of the amazing things I saw in my own journey through cancer was the church come alive in a way I had never seen before. For the first time in my life in the church, I was the one being prayed over. People were offering to bring meals, clean my house, give me rides to appointments or work, and sit in the hospital waiting room or during surgery or treatments. Most of all, they were giving me the spiritual encouragement to trust in Christ and continue on in my walk of faith.

While I was fighting my cancer there were people getting engaged, getting married, having babies, buying homes, and being honored. The same church walked in excitement with those who were going through those wonderful days. The church was willing to walk with each person in the church, regardless of the situation, and in all situations they gave God the glory.

I know this isn't true for all churches or all people. I saw my own share of fair-weather friends—those who were with me in the good times, but once those storm clouds billowed on the horizon they were gone. Sadly, this was true of some friends and even some in my church. That may represent the twenty-first-century church more than the church that rejoices and weeps together. Yet, I saw a movement of genuine, sincere, and authentic faith among so many in their walks with Christ. It was incredibly encouraging.

While I observed the church from a new and dearly cherished perspective, it caused me to pray for the church—not just my church or those believers in the United States, but the church throughout the entire world. I learned to pray for a genuine, sincere, authentic faith for each Christ-follower. You and I have seen plenty of people playing church. I dare say that we have seen their plastic faith: everything looks good on the outside but is falling apart on the inside, and they've deceived themselves about their great faith. I confess that I have done it before too. But what I saw in my suffering, to an even greater degree, was the depth of faith in so many.

Embracing your trial is a way of embracing the authentic faith that Christ wants all of us to have. You have been given an incredible gift of seeing your life and the Lord's church with new eyes and with a new perspective. Pray for the church that they may come alongside you, while you're in the valley, rejoice with those who are rejoicing and weep with those who are weeping. It's strange to say, but it truly is a wonderful thing to be in pain and hardship and to truly smile with fellow brothers and sisters in Christ—to rejoice and to weep at the same time. That's true faith.

When the trial is over, do not forget to walk with those who cared for you. So many have made sacrifices to be with you. While most don't expect anything in return—and they shouldn't do it for that reason—I pray you've developed deeper relationships that will be long-term, faithful friendships. At some point they're going to need your help and prayer. Through your trial you will be more than equipped to come alongside those who are weeping and those who are rejoicing.

Christ is going to work in the life of the church. He's calling you to work in the life of the church during your trial.

GOOD, NOT BAD?

*"But he said to her, 'You speak as one of the foolish women would speak. Shall we receive good from God, and shall we not receive evil?'
In all this Job did not sin with his lips" ~Job 2:10*

Job is one of the most unique and inspiring books in all of history and literature, bringing to light the sufferings all people go through. He lost all of his children, lost all of his wealth, and lost his position and respect in society within hours and days. You could say that he lost everything. Very early on in his trial, Job realized the place of God in the lives of people. After his wonderful wife (enter sarcasm) questions God and Job's faith in this calamity, Job replied, "Shall we receive good from God, and shall we not receive evil?" (As an aside for Job's wife, it's important to remember that just as Job lost his fortune, his home, his kids, so did she. Her reaction was so very human.)

Do you ever find in the church that people are quick to look at their material possessions, the number of children they have, or success in their job as a blessing from God? We are quick to ignore God when things are good and life is great. It's interesting to see how people change their tune when things go south. We're fast to blame God though when things turn against us. It's easy for people to try to find sin or a person's inadequacies when tough times come. We're quick to praise God in the good times but slow to see God's hand in the storm. We may even ignore God in the good times but wonder where He is— as if He had left.

Job understood that God had a hand in all the parts of his life—not just in the good but also in the bad. Job knew that God had a hand in the good life he lived before. He also knew that God had a major hand in taking it all away. Even though Satan brought about Job's calamity, God permitted Satan to take away his wealth and his children. Nothing happened in Job's life without God's permission and allowance, and nothing happens in your life without God allowing it to happen. God doesn't cause sin, but He can use the consequences of sin in our world for His own purposes and ultimate glory. He saw the greater good and

His greater purpose in giving Job this opportunity to be tested, and it's the same for your situation.

There is nothing that is happening to you that God is not aware of, that He did not allow, or that He does not control. God is ultimately sovereign in your life. He knows each intimate detail about you. He knows each decision you will make, and He knows the outcome of this struggle. He is the writer of your story, and you are a player in His story of redemption. As Hebrews 12:2 (NKJV) says, Jesus is "the author and finisher of our faith." He wrote your salvation, and He's writing your life story with each breath you take, because it's a part of His story.

NO GOD BESIDE ME

"See now that I, even I, am he, and there is no god beside me;
I kill and I make alive; I wound and I heal; and there is none
that can deliver out of my hand" ~Deuteronomy 32:39

With all we have in the Bible, it must be said that we have barely scratched the surface as to who God is. I think we'll be surprised when we go to heaven, by the totality of who God is. God is revealing Himself to the people of Israel in this passage from Deuteronomy. Because the people are surrounded by false gods and other distractions, the Lord wants to ensure that they know exactly who He is. The passage applies to us because we are distracted by our trial and our world, distracted by advice, or even distracted by false encouragement and the world's promises. God wants us to see Him, as He is, not a photoshopped description, but the reality of His existence and His character. He is very direct with Israel, just as He needs to be direct and simple with us.

There is no one who will faithfully and entirely walk the trial with you, except for God; He will walk each second with you. There is one God, one Lord, one Savior, and one faith. He declares that everything is under His control. He kills and makes alive, wounds and heals. God will direct each of your steps, each job interview, each doctor appointment, each conversation, and each teardrop. He knows each decision you will make and has full control over every part of your life, even when it seems the world is crashing in around you.

At this point, you do not know the end of your trial. The reality is you may never know. Rest in the fact that God does. He planned it, allowed it, even orchestrated it for His purpose. He knows the exact moment when it will end for you. Deliverance is in His hand and in the hands of no other. No one else can deliver you, heal you, or help you without God's direction and allowance. In God's timing your trial will end.

DELIVERANCE

"Because he holds fast to me in love, I will deliver him; I will protect him, because he knows my name. When he calls to me, I will answer him; I will be with him in trouble; I will rescue him and honor him. With long life I will satisfy him and show him my salvation" ~Psalm 91:14–16

You've been given one large decision to make in your present circumstances: Will you rely on yourself or hold fast to the Lord? This world is going to fail you, possessions will fail you, status will fail you, people will fail you, and the earthly solutions to the problems of this world will fail you. The only hope in your circumstances is to hold fast and cling to Christ. Notice that when you cling to Christ, He says, "I will deliver him." Christ-follower, God knows your name and all the intricacies and facets of your life far better than you ever will. He's promised to protect you, whether that end is what you want or what He wants—to the end.

God's immediate promise in verse 14 is deliverance. Deliverance takes many forms in this promise. It might be a new job, healing from sickness, or a restored relationship. Deliverance may also result in the loss of everything, including your life. Yet, God will deliver you, in His way, in His time. As your Savior, Christ has already delivered you from the worst thing that could ever happen to you—ever: an eternity separated from Him in hell because of your sin. It may be hard in the midst of your circumstances to latch on to that truth, but do, because just as God has delivered you from sin, He is going to deliver you from your struggle. He will do this even if deliverance means that you will be removed from this world and enter His presence, which truly would be the greatest deliverance you could have.

Look at the many promises of the Lord throughout your life that are listed in this passage. He first promises to protect you, which requires that He needs to be present in your life—another promise He fulfills in salvation. If He is present in your life, that means that He can hear your every cry, every plea, and every praise. Part of His answers to your prayers are the promises found in His Word. Lastly, in this passage God promises to rescue and to honor. God provides the rescue and deliverance. At the end of the trial God is going to honor you, not because of anything you did, but because of everything He did.

At the close of the passage the Lord says, "With long life I will satisfy him and show him my salvation." Your life on this earth is short, even if you live to be one hundred years old. God gives you long life in and through Himself. God is going to satisfy you with His presence from the moment of salvation through eternity. One of the things that God may be doing in your trial is taking your eyes and focus off this current life (and your present trial) so that you may see God's salvation at work in this life and in the life to come. It's bigger than any good this world could provide, and He has gifted you with this opportunity to turn your focus exclusively toward the Lord. So few people are given this great gift. You get the rare privilege, in your suffering, to see God at work. In the big and the small, God is able to show you His glory in and through your suffering.

FOURTEEN SONGS

"Is anyone among you suffering? Let him pray. Is anyone cheerful?
Let him sing praise" ~James 5:13

Music has a way of explaining human emotion in a completely different way than any words ever could. It has a way of taking our innermost thoughts and bringing them to light.

Music plays a big role in human life, and I pray there will be songs and albums that encourage you during your trial and bring some relief and escape in the middle of your storm—songs that draw you closer to the Lord. I'm not musical in any way, but in song these talented musicians have given such great comfort through their music.

Fourteen songs, among so many encouraging songs, stood out over my time with cancer and helped me define the trial, see the future in a different light, and learn to trust God more. These songs were such a gift during a dark time in my life that I pray you will find them helpful. I truly could not write any additional wisdom to these songs, though I will try to write some short commentary as they appear on the next few pages.

I have intentionally left the lyrics out of the entries so that you may listen to each song as the artist intended. All are easily accessible on the Internet. Hopefully you've already heard some of the songs before or have even sung them in your church or, as I do, in your car. I have included the artists' websites as well as the YouTube address if the artist has made a music video or posted the song.

Is it possible that someone in the midst of suffering can both pray and praise? My prayer for you is that you can pray in your suffering and praise God for the work that is at hand, your purity in Christ.

As David writes in Psalm 27:6: "And now my head shall be lifted up above my enemies all around me, and I will offer in his tent sacrifices with shouts of joy; I will sing and make melody to the LORD."

* * *

I have also created a playlist on Spotify under *anchoredinthestorm*. It
includes these fourteen songs as well as some others
that will center your thoughts and focus your heart on the Lord.

"BLESSINGS"

"More than that, we rejoice in our sufferings, knowing that suffering produces endurance, and endurance produces character, and character produces hope, and hope does not put us to shame, because God's love has been poured into our hearts through the Holy Spirit who has been given to us. For while we were still weak, at the right time Christ died for the ungodly" ~Romans 5:3–6

"Blessings" – by Laura Story

In our Christian society the word *blessing* means good things—the blessing of a job promotion, a new baby, a Hawaiian vacation. But does God have the same definition of blessing? Laura Story, in her song *Blessings*, took an opposite view of the word *blessings* and of our comfort with a partial understanding of the Lord's blessing of our lives.

Part of Story's song asks: *"What if trials of this life…the rain, the storms, the hardest nights…are your mercies in disguise?"*

Can you honestly look at your storm, your suffering, as a blessing? Is the Lord's mercy and grace upon you a blessing? In your mind, is your thinking of blessings as good things, or do you see God's work in your life—no matter the ease or difficulty—a blessing from His hand?

Through your trial, God is gifting you, His mercy and His patience over you. Story sings:

> *'Cause what if Your blessing comes through rain drops?*
> *What if Your healing comes through tears?*
> *What if a thousand sleepless nights*
> *   are what it takes to know You're near?*
> *What if the trials of this life are Your mercies in disguise?*

Story's song comes out of the trial her husband faced with his own brain tumor. No one said that our trials would be easy, but that doesn't mean they can't be a blessing. I pray you will see your trial as a blessing—maybe not today or tomorrow, but someday.

* * *

http://laurastorymusic.com

"GLORIOUS UNFOLDING"

"The plans of the heart belong to man, but the answer of the tongue is from the LORD. All the ways of a man are pure in his own eyes, but the LORD weighs the spirit. Commit your works to the LORD, and your plans will be established. The LORD has made everything for its purpose,
even the wicked for the day of trouble" ~Proverbs 16:1–4

"Glorious Unfolding" – by Steven Curtis Chapman

Isn't it true that so many of our days in the valley of our trials are spent thinking about and dwelling on our situation? It eats away at our soul and exhausts us. We long for peaceful sleep, yet in these struggles, sleep is so very hard to find.

Chapman starts off this amazing song with an exhortation to lay our heads down and rest in the sovereignty of our God. In God's sovereignty we can find peace and rest. He sings about how we thought our lives were going to be so different from how life currently is, and he is so right. We expected life to be different, circumstances to be different, the outcome to be different. We expected so much more, so much better. But it's not, and here we are. We expected to be one of those people who succeeded in life in every way while also growing in the grace and knowledge of our God with minimal effort and pain. But that is not our story, nor is it God's story.

The last line of the first stanza says, "There's so much of the story that's still yet to unfold." Your trial doesn't define you, because Christ does. Your story is far from over. As a Christ-follower you have an eternal story that's yet to be written. Even if you are on your deathbed, your story is not over. This is not the end, but it is most certainly the blessing.

Chapman calls this song the *"Glorious Unfolding"*—the glorious unfolding of God's work in your life for His great purpose and greater glory. Your life on this earth "is just the beginning of the beginning," a small portion of your entire existence. We cannot see our lives within the totality of God's story. In the scheme of eternity our lives on this

161

earth are very short. Your life is just the beginning of a very great beginning in eternity, of which there is no end.

You have a glorious future ahead; will you allow God to unfold His work in your life so He can write your story?

* * *

http://stevencurtischapman.com

https://www.youtube.com/watch?v=GKMjEvF2Fkw

"OCEANS"

*"But immediately Jesus spoke to them, saying,
'Take heart; it is I. Do not be afraid'" ~Matthew 14:27*

"Oceans" – by Hillsong United

Just as Jesus called Peter out of the boat onto the crashing waves of the Sea of Galilee, God has a unique call upon your life, a very special call. However, God's call for you is not very different than from what His was of Peter. His call for you is to leave behind the calm beach, the carefree life everyone else is living on the beach, to enter the shallow water, to leave it behind, and to head into the deep and crashing waves so that you may meet Him there. Your faith can no longer be shallow, like that of so many Christians who desire to avoid trials and who fear the storms that will come. God is calling you to the depths of who He is so that you may forsake this world and walk with Him in His grace and mercy. Your faith will now be grounded, steadfast, and anchored to the rock that is Christ.

So many believers are content enjoying the surf and sun on the beach, thinking that this is what it means to be a Christian. But rare is the person who "gets it" and is willing to take that step of faith in God's call to "walk upon the waters," however hard that might be. In your trial, you are choosing to give up lying on the beach for bracing the ship in the storm. You are choosing to give up this world for the sake of knowing Christ. Truly, what a glorious opportunity the Lord is gifting to you in these dark times. At the end of this trial, whether in this life or the next, you will have travelled where few people, including many believers, have dared to go. God has called you to a different life, completely abandoned to the will of God to be a part of bringing God great glory and working in the kingdom to expand and strengthen it.

Fun happens on the shore. True adventure, strength, and courage happen away from the shallows and the shoreline. Only in the depths of the ocean and the distances from land does one truly learn to sail under the guidance of the Lord.

Will you take the step into the stormy sea to see God do a wondrous work in your life?

* * *

http://hillsong.com/store/products/music/united/oceans-ep

https://www.youtube.com/watch?v=N2PNTq_-mZs

"SUN AND MOON"

*"And take the helmet of salvation and the sword of the Spirit,
which is the word of God" ~Ephesians 6:17*

"Sun and Moon" – by Phil Wickham

Phil Wickham sings in *"Sun and Moon"*, *"And if this is war then I'm gonna
draw my sword, this time I know what I'm fighting for."*

Whether you know it or not, you are at war, and as a Christ-follower
you have always been at war. You may be at war with discouragement,
unemployment, a crushed heart, health issues, lost opportunities, failed
relationships, depression, or a broken life. This trial may be a war for
your soul. Satan and his ilk want to get you at your weakest, to make you
doubt the goodness of God, so that you will question God's work and
lose faith. You are at war in so many parts of your life. You may never
know the full extent of the spiritual warfare going on around you.

Do you know what you are fighting for? You are fighting, with Jesus
by your side, for your faith, your family, your relationships, and the
salvation and encouragement of the souls who are watching you and
fighting with you and for you. No doubt, my friend, war is raging all
around you in every way. How are you going to respond?

Take up the sword of truth, the Word of God, and fight like you
have never fought before.

* * *

http://www.philwickham.com

https://www.youtube.com/watch?v=8ukIwjws88E

"SUN AND MOON" – PART 2

"For you have delivered my soul from death, yes, my feet from falling, that I may walk before God in the light of life" ~Psalm 56:13

"Sun and Moon" – by Phil Wickham

Later in Phil Wickham's *"Sun and Moon"* he sings, *"God, I wanna let you know I want everything you are. I'm waiting for the morning light to show a fire in the dark."* As all who walk in the valley, you are no doubt in a very dark place wherever you are in the midst of your battle. The valley of suffering is not one where you can see the sun. Even the light from the sun is hard to come by. It's dark; it's scary. Every day, like clockwork, the sun makes its crest on the horizon, whether we see it or not. Without fail the sun will shine. Even when the darkest clouds are overhead, the sun is shining brilliantly above them. You can rest in the truth that God is shining in your life, even if you can't see Him. There has never been a night without its dawn nor a dawn without its night. Yet, God graces all mankind with the light and the dark. The same is happening to you. You're in the dark right now, but you serve a God who works all things for your good in His time. The light will no doubt come, but the timing is not for us to know.

However, it is for us to remain faithful, for God has proven His own faithfulness to us. As a Christian you ultimately want all that God has for you in Christ. Part of having that happen is to go through trials big and small, to make you more like Christ in every way. As Wickham sings, do you really want to know everything of who God is?

* * *

http://www.philwickham.com

https://www.youtube.com/watch?v=8ukIwjws88E

"IN CHRIST ALONE"

"For there is one God, and there is one mediator between God and men, the man Christ Jesus" ~1 Timothy 2:5

"In Christ Alone" – by Keith Getty and Stuart Townsend

Out of so many of the songs sung in our churches, so few declare the life, death, and resurrection of Christ as succinctly as *"In Christ Alone."* That doesn't make them bad songs, but it's incredible that this song has been sung during communion, at Christmas, on Good Friday, at Easter, and, I pray, now, in your valley.

Every section of this song relates part of Christ's life with ours and declares how we can identify with Christ as Christ-followers. We can relate to Christ in His love, in His death, in His purchase of us, and in our destiny with Him in heaven.

There is no enemy and no defeat for the person who trusts in Christ alone.

* * *

https://www.gettymusic.com/hymns-inchristalone.aspx

"BE STILL"

"Be still, and know that I am God. I will be exalted among the nations, I will be exalted in the earth!" ~Psalm 46:10

"Be Still" – by The Fray

You may find that during your trial there will be many sleepless nights and many exhausting days. It may be hard to "be still" and rest in anything or anyone. The Fray brings us a song that I've ended up singing to myself to remind me of the Lord's presence and power so many times. They may not be identified as a Christian band, but there is no doubt they use Psalm 46:10 as inspiration for this beautiful song.

When I listen to the song I hear the words of God from the psalm come through, and when I think of the line, *"Be still and know I am,"* it reminds me of God's name in the Old Testament: "I AM," or "I AM WHO I AM." It's a great reminder of His power, self-existence, grace, and sovereignty upon the people of His creation. It's also a great reminder of His presence. His name doesn't say, "I was," or "I will be." His name is "I am"—always present in the here and now. The Lord is not a god who was and will not return, nor is He a god who is busy with his own pursuits. But He is God, who is with you always. As Jesus says in the Great Commission, "Behold, I am with you always to the end of the age." *(Matthew 28:20)*

Be still and rest that you serve a God who has everything under control.

* * *

http://www.thefray.com

168

"STORM"

"My heart is in anguish within me; the terrors of death have fallen upon me. Fear and trembling come upon me, and horror overwhelms me. And I say, "Oh, that I had wings like a dove!
I would fly away and be at rest; yes, I would wander far away;
I would lodge in the wilderness; I would hurry to find a shelter from the raging wind and tempest" ~Psalm 55:4–8

"Storm" – by Lifehouse

David, in Psalm 55, seemed to capture in words the thoughts and emotions of present suffering. He described his own conflict as anguish, terror, and horror—the same words that may go through your mind. And like us, David would gladly flee his trials, like a bird, to find rest. I can't speak for you, but this song by Lifehouse encapsulates feelings that I could not express with my own words, just as David's words explain feelings I couldn't verbalize. I do not know if Lifehouse is identified as a Christian group or not, but this song resonates so distinctly with us in our trials and speaks to a contrast of two people and two perspectives of suffering.

Do you see the contrast between living on our own and living with God? Living on our own during our trials is very difficult. We can barely keep our head above the waves, treading water is difficult, and what's going on is completely beyond any understanding of ours.

Yet, think about the contrast of walking this trial with God. You will walk on the waters. God is going to catch you if you fall, and the person walking with God knows that everything will be all right. In your suffering, can you say, "Everything will be all right?" Can you honestly say that? Do you honestly believe that?

You get to choose which person you will be. Are you going to be the person barely treading water, sinking lower and lower after each successive wave? Or are you going to be the person that Jesus calls to take His hand and walk on the water? Both are hard choices. Choosing to go it alone though, without Christ, means barely surviving. Choosing

Jesus means giving up yourself, your rights, and your trial to His control. In the end you will not just survive, you will thrive in your relationship and faith in Christ.

Take His hand. Go out into the storm.

* * *

http://lifehousemusic.com/music/

"WORN"

"Come to me, all who labor and are heavy laden, and I will give you rest. Take my yoke upon you, and learn from me, for I am gentle and lowly in heart, and you will find rest for your souls.
For my yoke is easy, and my burden is light" ~Matthew 11:28–30

"Worn" – by Tenth Avenue North

Whatever your trial is, the reality is that we all have broken lives, and there is only One who can truly heal all the hurts we carry with us on this dark journey. You and I have looked earlier at this world we live in. This world is dying, and we are a people who will physically die. Life is hard, and there are so many days, even on good days, when our days are dark, breathing is difficult, and there is no energy or life in us.

The reason our world is dying—the reason you and I die—the reason we have trials is because of our sin. Your sin may not have caused your trial, but the difficulties in your life are because of sin. God, who is perfect, works within the realities of this world to bring about our good and His glory. He allows suffering to show His strength, His glory, and Himself. He is light, and in your darkness of sin and suffering He shows Himself the brightest.

Before there was a star in the sky or breath in the lungs, God knew men and women would sin, plunging this world into spiritual darkness. Before the world was created, God had a plan, as He always does—even when it appears He doesn't. The Lord cannot be where sin dwells, which means that we have a broken relationship with Him. Before sin, Adam and Eve had a great relationship with God. Sin ruined that relationship. God wants to be intimately involved in His creation. He wants to know you, wants to help you, and most of all, He wants you to be in His family and a part of His kingdom. With sin in our world, a relationship with God is an impossibility, bringing death into this world and the eternal death of our souls.

However, before creation He had a plan to heal the relationship between Him and us, to destroy sin, and to defeat eternal death. His

171

plan for you and me was to get rid of sin, which involved death—the death of His Son, Jesus Christ. Jesus gladly came to this world to die for you and me so that we may be reconciled to Him and so that He could give us new life. In His death, Christ brought life.

How do you get this life? All you need to do is to agree with God that you are a sinner and that you have a broken relationship with God. Submit yourself to Christ as Lord and Savior. It means surrendering your life and embracing the life He has in store for His children. Doing so is not easy, but the life therein makes it all worth it. And it makes this trial you're in worth it all too.

Despite the pain and suffering, have you embraced Christ as your Savior? Have you embraced the plan of Christ for your life?

* * *

http://www.tenthavenuenorth.com

https://www.youtube.com/watch?v=zulKcYItKIA

"WORN" – PART 2

"Behold, he is coming with the clouds, and every eye will see him, even those who pierced him, and all the tribes of the earth will wail on account of him. Even so. Amen" ~Revelation 1:7

"Worn" – by Tenth Avenue North

During a trial the days are long and dark. Our breathing is heavy and labored. Our energy is low, and our will to press on is very weak. The goals and purpose for our trials are absent or ambiguous. The trial itself is difficult, but so is surviving and living through the trial.

What can be done about this? Who can help? The answer comes once again to Christ. Christ is already in this, and He's already with you. The song *"Worn"* is a declaration that you can't take on the challenges of living in this world. It's a call to see redemption ultimately fulfilled in your life.

Yes, as Christians we are redeemed, but the effects of sin still take their toll on us, especially during trials. As joyous as our walks with Christ are, the weight of this world weighs upon our souls, and we cry out, not for salvation, but to see Christ and His will fulfilled and completed for His followers.

Take heart, because the day is coming when it will be so, and we will see the world fully as God created it to be, and even better, we'll see Him.

* * *

http://www.tenthavenuenorth.com

https://www.youtube.com/watch?v=zulKcYItKIA

"LIVE LIKE THAT"

"Whoever says he abides in him ought to walk in the same way in which he walked" ~1 John 2:6

"Live Like That" – by Sidewalk Prophets

Have you ever thought of what people will say at your funeral? Yes, it's a sober, dark, self-absorbed question, but there is much beneath the shallowness of the question, because it is really asking, "What kind of life did you live? What kind of life are you presently living? Was your life worth it all, or was it a waste?" Those questions take the original question to a deeper, less selfish level and allow you to take a look back at your life to evaluate where you've been and where you are going. But you still have breath in your lungs, and in your trial you are given the amazing gift of introspection. How do you want to live your life? How do you want to be remembered? How does Christ impact the life ahead of you?

Sidewalk Prophets takes this song and gives us inspiration to live a life that honors Christ. Some of the topics they sing about are phrased as questions: *"Was I Jesus to those in need?"*

Are you willing to give your all for the sake of Christ? Is there anything holding you back from living your entire life for Christ? Does every breath you take focus on Christ? Do you want to share Christ with every person you meet? How is your worship—not in song, but in living life? Are you holding back from living every aspect of your life for Christ and for His kingdom? Are you living like that? Maybe I should ask: Are you ready to live like that?

* * *

http://www.sidewalkprophets.com

https://www.youtube.com/watch?v=GfosSggwQS0

174

"SHOULDERS"

"Bear one another's burdens,
and so fulfill the law of Christ" ~Galatians 6:2

"Shoulders" – by For King and Country

Are your shoulders burdened by the weight of your journey? Does this weight leave you out of breath, ready to collapse? Is it a burden that carries into your sleep and haunts your dreams? Is life confusing, and you don't know where to turn? Are you trying to find some sort of comfort yet aren't finding it anywhere? When life is falling apart and you have more questions than answers, where do you turn?

There is only One who can answer your deepest questions; only One who can carry you when you can no longer walk; only One whose help is freely given. The only answer is in the Lord Jesus Christ through His sacrifice. True, abiding, and lasting help comes only from one source—the Lord, and no other. He created this world; He knows it best; and—dare it be said? —He knows more about you than even you do. It takes a lot to give your life and ambitions over to Him, but who better to give it all over to than Him?

David writes in Psalm 55:22: "Cast your burden on the LORD, and he will sustain you; he will never permit the righteous to be moved."

* * *

http://www.forkingandcountry.com

https://www.youtube.com/watch?v=TfiYWaeAcRw

"HOW SWEET THE SOUND"

"Every word of God proves true; he is a shield to those
who take refuge in him" ~Proverbs 30:5

"How Sweet the Sound" – by Citizen Way

You and I have asked ourselves: Where is God in all this? What is the purpose of our suffering? One of God's purposes is to walk with you to help you recognize His presence. It may feel like you are all alone, but right beside you is Christ, who is stronger and greater than any force on this earth.

His presence should be a comfort to your soul. Before the Lord, as He walks with you, you will be silent. It is He who is your healing and shelter during these trying times. He is a shield about you!

* * *

http://citizenwaymusic.com

https://www.youtube.com/watch?v=IFqxwW21bxw

"THROUGH ALL OF IT"

"Yet he is actually not far from each one of us, for 'In him we live and move and have our being" ~*Acts 17:27–28*

"Through All of It" – by Colton Dixon

The first few lines sum up so much of our lives: the choices we've made, the troubled times we live in—these things are the story of our lives. Part of Colton Dixon's song goes on: *"I have won, and I have lost."* As we look back on our lives, we can see the good times, and now we are in the bad times. Truly life has been a journey, and truly in our lives we've been on the mountaintops and in the valleys.

Dixon's chorus echoes the phrase, *"Through all of it you have been my God."* In every heartbeat and breath of your life, in every sunrise and every sunset, the one consistency is that God is with you, through it all.

Sometimes He's loud and you see His work, at other times He's quiet, working behind the scenes. But He is always there with you, His child—through all of it!

* * *

http://www.coltondixon.com

https://www.youtube.com/watch?v=ZnuGXvO_l8w

"NEED YOU NOW (HOW MANY TIMES)"

"Will you restrain yourself at these things, O LORD? Will you keep silent, and afflict us so terribly?" ~ Isaiah 64:12

"Need You Now (How Many Times)" – by Plumb

Isaiah, in the passage above, asks a pressing question for us in our trials. The same question may be asked when prayers go unanswered or when we are unaware of God's hand in our lives. This is such a human question and one that stems from our limited understanding. So many times in our lives God is very quiet or silent. That doesn't mean He is not answering prayers or working behind the scenes.

Our trials can be devastating; we may have lost a great many things. Plumb seems to have written a song that resonates with the desperation that dwells so deeply in our hearts. The wonderful thing about our relationship with Christ is that He wants to hear every part of our hearts: our praise of Him, our worries, the good and the bad. In prayer we communicate our hearts to God.

So in your trial, cry out to Him. He is longing to hear your voice and to work in your life. I pray that you will realize what the prophet Zephaniah said, "The LORD your God is in your midst, a mighty one who will save; he will rejoice over you with gladness; he will quiet you by his love; he will exult over you with loud singing." (*Zephaniah 3:17*) He is the mighty One who saves.

* * *

http://plumbmusic.net

https://www.youtube.com/watch?v=Y9CjYvQDDIo

"EVEN IF"

"Not that I am speaking of being in need, for I have learned in whatever situation I am to be content" ~Philippians 4:11

"Even If" – by Kutless

Most likely you picked up this book or were given this book because you were in a trial or were preparing to enter a trial. I'm sure you have thought, as I have: What if my trial doesn't end? What if the suffering doesn't end? They are questions. Many people are afflicted with long-lasting medical issues, unending financial problems that drastically change their way of life, or a broken relationship that is never healed or restored. These are real possibilities in our lives as well.

If you face an extended or lifelong trial, how does your relationship with the Lord stay the same or change? Even if the healing doesn't come, how are you going to think of and respond to Christ?

Kutless's song, *"Even If,"* brings to mind many of these questions and our possible responses if that healing we expect doesn't come. There are great truths to dwell upon and consider in our suffering.

If the healing doesn't come, could you say, as Paul writes in Philippians 4:11–13, "For I have learned in whatever situation I am to be content. I know how to be brought low, and I know how to abound. In any and every circumstance, I have learned the secret of facing plenty and hunger, abundance and need. I can do all things through him who strengthens me?"

* * *

http://www.kutless.com

https://www.youtube.com/watch?v=HqOkZiOb9u0

THE GREAT SHEPHERD

"The LORD is my shepherd; I shall not want. He makes me lie down in green pastures. He leads me beside still waters. He restores my soul. He leads me in paths of righteousness for his name's sake. Even though I walk through the valley of the shadow of death, I will fear no evil for you are with me; your rod and your staff, they comfort me. You prepare a table before me in the presence of my enemies; you anoint my head with oil; my cup overflows. Surely goodness and mercy shall follow me all the days of my life, and I shall dwell in the house of the LORD forever" ~Psalm 23

Psalm 23 is often spoken or read at funerals, and rightly so. There are many allusions to rest and peace beyond the life of this world. The call of death may be upon you, as it one day will be for all of us, but today let's look and see what Psalm 23 has for us in the land of the living. Let's discover what David is writing to us in this psalm to help focus us during our trial. The first three verses contain so much that pertains to the plights of our suffering. We are learning how the Lord is our shepherd over our lives and trials. The reality of sheep is they are stupid, make terrible decisions, and are incapable of living their lives without leadership and direction.

Wait a minute, doesn't that sound like us? I can't speak for you, but I can be stupid at times; I make terrible decisions, and I am also utterly incapable of living this life entirely on my own.

The Lord wants you as one of His sheep; He wants to provide you with leadership and direction. He wants to care for you, to take you places you've never imagined, over paths and roads you would never have chosen on your own. With God as your Shepherd it's guaranteed that many great adventures, easy and hard, await you. Notice the things He does as your Shepherd: He forces rest upon you, restores and leads you, and prepares a place for you to dwell in His house. In the turmoil and uncertainty of your current circumstances, He is preparing and delivering these things for you.

A good way to describe how I felt when I was walking through my cancer journey was that I was walking through the valley of the shadow of death. Diagnosing my cancer was extremely difficult, and having something very rare, I thought for sure that death would be upon me soon. You will someday enter this same valley—or maybe you're already there. We will all face death at some point. It's a valley of darkness and loneliness, and for some the shadow of death is very much upon them. In this valley, though, the psalmist declares that he will fear no evil. How is it possible that he fears no evil when he is seemingly facing death? The answer lies in his knowledge that the Lord is with him. He may be walking alone without anyone by his side, but the truth is that God is with him with each step he takes.

David, who is in the middle of his own trial, gives us incredible insight into how God works. He says that God has prepared a table overflowing with goodness in the midst of his enemies. While God is fighting David's enemies, the Lord is causing him to sit, rest, eat, and be refreshed in the presence of the Lord. In the midst of your own trial, God is preparing a table for you to be refreshed and energized for the rest of the fight in the valley. This table may be a real table in heaven. Perhaps it signifies that He is going to bring around you His truth and His people so that you may be encouraged and press on.

Did you notice that we never see David leave the valley of the shadow of death? His trial continues on, even after he finished penning this. The reality of our trials is that while we are on this earth, we will face trials many times—both large and small. Yet, what God does when we are saved and become Christ-followers is to prepare a place for us in His presence—a place that is going to last and that the troubles of this world cannot shake.

The place of peace is always with Christ, no matter what is going on in our lives and in this world.

SUFFICIENT FOR YOU

"But he said to me, 'My grace is sufficient for you,
for my power is made perfect in weakness,'
…so that the power of Christ may rest upon me.
For the sake of Christ, then, I am content with weaknesses, insults, hardships,
persecutions, and calamities.
For when I am weak, then I am strong" ~2 Corinthians 12:9–10

God can do absolutely anything He wants to; He has that kind of power. Think about the vastness of the universe. Yeah, God did that. Take a look at the cells of our bodies. Yeah, God did that too. God can do it all, however He wants to do it; everything is His. Nothing is outside of His control and power.

Our trials and our weaknesses are the perfect opportunity for God's power to be used mightily, for His glory and our benefit, as well as for the benefit of those who are fighting alongside us. One of the interesting things about Paul's phrasing is that God's power is perfect in weakness. He's not saying that God's power isn't perfect, but that our weaknesses are where His power most shines and works most effectively, where He is most glorified through this use of His power. You can rest in your trial because His power is upon you, and He is working for your good.

Paul took a fascinating view at the trials of this life and the specific trials he faced. He said that he was content with the weaknesses that went along with human suffering because they showed the power of Christ, and in Christ he was strong. Our weaknesses display the power of God as a bright light in the midst of the darkest night.

As John Piper writes, "Sometimes He makes seemingly strong people weaker, so that the divine power will be most evident." You've seen your strength decline, but it's all for God and His glory.

Piper continues: "Living by faith in God's grace means being satisfied with all that God is for us in Christ. Therefore, faith will not shrink back from what reveals and magnifies all that God is for us in Jesus. That is what our own weakness and suffering does."

Your trial is an opportunity for you to display God's majesty.

* * *

http://solidjoys.desiringgod.org/en/devotionals/
our-weakness-reveals-his-worth

LOVED EVEN MORE

"I will give him to the LORD *all the days of his life"* ~ *1 Samuel 1:11*

First Samuel chapters 1 and 2 tell the story of a woman named Hannah and her great sacrifice to the Lord. Hannah is a good wife with a good husband. Her husband had two wives, Hannah and Peninnah. He showed favor to Hannah because he loved her. His other wife was blessed with motherhood and the children of her womb, but still Hannah was barren—without children—and she was desperate to have children of her own. Even more, she was desperate for her relationship with the Lord and for however the Lord wanted to use the child He may someday bless her with. In the poverty of barrenness, she prayed that if the Lord allowed her to conceive she would dedicate the child to the Lord.

She prayed, "O LORD of hosts, if you will indeed look on the affliction of your servant and remember me and not forget your servant, but will give to your servant a son, then I will give him to the Lord all the days of his life." (v. 11) The Lord answered her prayer. Hannah conceived and gave birth to a son. Now she was conflicted. Would Hannah live up to what she had prayed? She asked for a child, and the Lord answered, but now Hannah was required to give the child over to the work of the Lord, for whatever the Lord had in mind.

Hannah, just like you, spent hours agonizing over this decision. She had longed and prayed for this child for years and years. The Lord answered and gave her a son, but now Hannah had to fulfill her promise to Him. By the grace of God she was given the strength to do so.

Like Abraham with his son Isaac, Hannah was challenged to sacrifice her son. She was not challenged to take his life, like Abraham had been with Isaac, but she must choose to give her son over to the High Priest in service to the Lord—for the rest of his life. Hannah would see her son from time to time, but this promised child would not be a daily, regular part of her life. He would commit every aspect of his life to the sake of the Lord.

The child's name was Samuel, whose name meant, "name of God." From birth this child was destined and called by God for God's specific purpose. He would anoint Saul the first king of Israel. He would also remove Saul from the throne and give David the monarchy, as was the will of the Lord. While Israel was not always faithful to the Lord, under Samuel's role, as prophet, he always worked to bring God's people back to Him.

Hannah's story, in 1 Samuel, is very much like that of Rachel and Jacob in Genesis, as well as of Abraham's own desire for an heir. You may relate to Hannah's story. You may be childless; you may have lost a child to miscarriage, you may be divorced and long for your children to be with you, you may not have talked to your child in years, or you had a child and he or she died. You may have no children, yet you still long for them. But in your trial the Lord has asked for everything you have, including yourself and all of your desires. In your tribulation, God is requiring something of you. It may be your child, your job, your house, your family, relationships, comfort, strength, or health. You have something precious to you that you're holding on to with tight fists, and what the Lord is doing is calling for these things so that He can be bigger in your life than these. He wants you to bow down before His throne without the distractions of this world calling your heart away from Him.

Hannah loved Samuel very much, but she loved her Lord even more and found it a blessing to work alongside the Lord's will and the Lord's plan for Israel. Hannah was unaware of the influence her son—and her sacrifice—would have on the people of Israel and on the Messiah. Just as Hannah was unaware, we so often are unaware of the great things that will come from the sacrifices in our suffering. God certainly works in mysteriously awesome ways!

THE MINISTRY OF OTHERS

"We who are strong have an obligation to bear with the failings of the weak, and not to please ourselves. Let each of us please his neighbor for his good to build him up" ~Romans 15:1–2

Often we think of ministry as doing something official at church: working with children, going to prayer night, cleaning the kitchen, or any other official program at the church. Yes, that's ministry, but it's a very small view of the ministry Christ had in mind. Ministry is found all over the place in the Christian life: in how we conduct ourselves, in our conversations with Christ-followers and future Christ-followers, and in how we display Christ to a hurting and dying world. Ministry is found in just sitting with a hurting friend, in praying over someone, in sharing a meal, or in giving an encouraging word. Ministry is so much broader than any program developed by humans in the church. Truly, ministry is life!

In your trial there will be people who will want to help you in whatever way they can. It might be something practical like preparing a meal, washing your car, cleaning your house, or something like sitting quietly with you in the hospital in the early morning hours. For them it is an opportunity to minister to you and to bring glory to God—a way of displaying Christ to you and others.

Just as you have had a lot to learn, the people who are ministering to you also have a lot to learn, and ministry is a way they can learn through your journey. Allow people to come into your life and into your home on this journey. This may be a challenge to you, because it's hard being vulnerable or saying that you have needs. Be wise though, because too many people can be a burden that will add to the weight of your trial. For many who are walking with you, it is their joy to serve you and the Lord in this ministry opportunity, but make sure to develop boundaries to protect yourself. Too much ministry can be quite draining, and you need your physical strength. If you need some peace and quiet, let others know. They'll understand. But don't be afraid to ask for help.

You'll find that believers and unbelievers alike will want to minister to you. Allow all who desire to serve you, to serve in whatever way they can. Christians can be strengthened in helping you, and unbelievers can see Christ in you and in other believers walking with you. They're the ones who need Christ, and being with you at mealtime or in the hospital is an opportunity for you to share Christ with them. You never know how God is going to use those interactions to spread His kingdom. There are many who may be saved by seeing Christ in your storm.

Right now, your trial is your ministry.

RECEIVE WHAT IS PROMISED

"But recall the former days when, after you were enlightened, you endured a hard struggle with sufferings, sometimes being publicly exposed to reproach and affliction, and sometimes being partners with those so treated. For you had compassion on those in prison, and you joyfully accepted the plundering of your property, since you knew that you yourselves had a better possession and an abiding one. Therefore do not throw away your confidence, which has a great reward. For you have need of endurance, so that when you have done the will of God you may receive what is promised. For, 'Yet a little while and the coming one will come and will not delay, but my righteous one shall live by faith, and if he shrinks back, my soul has no pleasure in him.' But we are not of those who shrink back and are destroyed, but of those who have faith
and preserve their souls" ~Hebrews 10:32–39

The author of Hebrews reminded readers of the struggles they endured in the past, and he reminded them of what they experienced and learned. He wrote: "You joyfully accepted the plundering of your property, since you knew that you yourselves had a better possession and an abiding one." He recounted the problems they may have faced—like many of the people he wrote about in Hebrews 11—and reminded them why they endured.

They endured their sufferings because they had something better to hold on to—something better than anything they could imagine. What they possessed was Christ. Unlike our material possessions, Christ endures. He's God, so He's going to be around a while. They were willing to sacrifice present short-term comforts for the sake of Christ and for what He is accomplishing for His kingdom through their plights. The author wrote: "For you have need of endurance, so that when you have done the will of God you may receive what is promised." Remember that God's ultimate promise to you as a Christ-follower is Himself. He is the reward for enduring to the end. Is there any greater reward than Christ Himself?

At the end of this passage, the author said, "But we are not of those who shrink back and are destroyed, but of those who have faith and preserve their souls." God allowed this trial because His people willingly accepted and embraced His call on their lives, whatever that entailed.

It is He who gives you the courage and strength to face every day and the struggles that each day may bring. You have placed your faith in Christ, and He will deliver you from the trial and will preserve and strengthen your soul.

A LASTING COVENANT

"I will make with them an everlasting covenant, that I will not turn away from doing good to them. And I will put the fear of me in their hearts, that they may not turn from me" ~Jeremiah 32:40

A covenant is a promise—one where the person making the covenant will face severe judgment if the covenant is broken. God is promising here that He will do good to them, to those He made the promise to—it is His covenant to His people. Christ-follower, God made this promise to you. He is not going to turn away from you today, tomorrow, or any day. He is with you to the end, and His covenants last through eternity; they will never end. He is working from this point on. By the way, God is never exhausted and is never tired. He may have rested on the seventh day, but it was to reflect on what He created, not because He was fatigued.

It's hard in the midst of difficult circumstances to think of how God is doing you good, but He is. He is bringing you closer to Him so that you are wholly dependent on Him. It is the greatest good you could have in this world. He is going to work good for you, to whatever end He wills, until He grows tired, which he never will for the sake of His children.

All the struggles of this life are to bring you to God, to allow you to see Him work, so that, in the end, you may hold on to God and not turn away from Him. He is not going to turn away from you at any point in this life. In time the trial will end. You will be close to God, and you'll be walking in the covenant relationship through salvation into eternity.

The goal of this trial is so that you will grow closer to the Lord and not turn away from Him.

TO TELL OF HIS WORKS

"Whom have I in heaven but you? And there is nothing on earth that I desire besides you. My flesh and my heart may fail, but God is the strength of my heart and my portion forever. For behold, those who are far from you shall perish; you put an end to everyone who is unfaithful to you. But for me it is good to be near God; I have made the Lord GOD my refuge, that I may tell of all your works" ~Psalm 73:25–28

Sharing testimonies should always be an encouraging time, whether it is one on one, in a small group, or from the pulpit. We each have different lives, and God seems to work in each life differently. The story of how God brings us to saving faith in Christ is always a fascinating one and is always glorious.

Your current trial is now part of your testimony. It reflects God's work in your life beyond salvation, displaying your weakness and God's greatness. The purpose of your trial is as it says at the end of Psalm 73: "that [you] may tell of [His] works."

The psalmist David knew exactly what you're going through. He knew each difficult breath, each deep heartache. It seemed like the world had abandoned him, yet God gave him an amazing perspective. In his loneliness and abandonment he clung to God. For the psalmist, everything had been taken away. He told of his body wasting away because of this trial. Yet, in his pain and weakness, God took center stage, bringing him into a closer relationship with the Lord.

Your trial may be small, or it may be big, but remember that from here on out you are to speak of how God has worked in your life. Just as He did with the psalmist, God is working in your pain to enhance your testimony, so others may see God's work in your life to expand and strengthen the kingdom.

UPWARD CALL OF GOD

"Not that I have already obtained this or am already perfect, but I press on to make it my own, because Christ Jesus has made me His own. Brothers, I do not consider that I have made it my own.
But one thing I do: forgetting what lies behind and straining forward to what lies ahead. I press on toward the goal for the prize of the upward call of God in Jesus Christ" ~Philippians 3:12–14

Paul made a few admissions that displayed his humility and help give a focus to steer us in the right direction when life seems to turn upside down. In this passage, Paul admitted that he was not perfect. And if Paul, of all people, isn't perfect, neither are we. Yes, in our difficulties God is refining us as a refiner purifies precious metals from impure metals. He is making us more like Christ through the flames of suffering. This work of God continues until we're fully purified in our entrance to heaven. Each part of this journey is moving our hearts from the things we love in this world and turning our hearts more and more toward Christ. Perfection will come, but only in God's time, my friend. Only at the end of our days, when we are present before Christ, will perfection be a reality for us.

Paul is working on his own Christlikeness, his own faith in Christ through the treacherous times he faced. He was able, just like you, to look at his life, see his sin, and repent before the Lord. He was pursuing Christ just as Christ was pursuing him. And it's the same with you. You are pursuing Christ in this trial, and Christ is with you, ever present in your trial, pursuing you. He's pursuing you more than you could ever pursue Him.

So many times our past is a hindrance to our growing in Christ. We hold on to our past, it anchors us in a time that we can't change or go back to. It's hard to let go of the past; it is a part of who we are, whether good or bad. Paul was one who looked on his past with shame. Some of the things he did were terrible, including killing many Christians. He was ashamed, but he was not going to let what he couldn't change hinder his progress and future in Christ. He knew he'd been forgiven by Christ and loved Christ more than the shame of his past. Do you?

Paul was willing to forsake his past for the greater pursuit of His Lord and Savior, Jesus Christ. He was going to press on toward heaven with all he had.

The ultimate goal and reward of our life with Jesus is Jesus Himself, a relationship and life with Christ into eternity. Paul came to the understanding that Christ *was* the reward—a greater reward than all the wealth of this world and even the wealth of heaven. Paul had the right perspective, and he was willing to sacrifice everything in the pursuit of Christ.

Like Paul, we are called to yearn, strive, and endure for the great future we have ahead of us in Christ. As written by the author of Hebrews: "Let us run with endurance the race that is set before us, looking to Jesus…" (Hebrews 12:1–2). You may not have lived for Christ in the past, but the present is the perfect time to do so. The prize is truly the upward call of Christ on your life!

FAITH AS VALUE TO GOD

"But for me it is good to be near God; I have made the Lord GOD my refuge, that I may tell of all your works" ~Psalm 73:28

John Piper writes in one of his *Solid Joys* devotional entries, "God so values our wholehearted faith that He will, graciously, take away everything else in the world that we might be tempted to rely on—even life itself. His aim is that we grow deeper and stronger in our confidence that He Himself will be all we need."

The Lord so greatly loves you; even before time began He loved you. And He would do anything for you to bring you closer to Him, including allowing trials. It sounds strange, doesn't it—allowing you pain and discomfort to grow closer to Him? That's like a friend punching you so you'll be better friends. But God has greater wisdom in this than we can understand. Your heart, you see, is torn between this world and Him. To have you rely completely upon Him, you are sometimes given opportunities to suffer, to show the failings of your trust so that you will trust Him always. He wants to bring you to the breaking point so that you need nothing in this world but Christ.

Earlier in the devotional, Piper writes that in our sufferings we are building spiritual muscle. Our physical muscles and stamina may be fading—quickly—but in your trial you are building spiritual muscle through faith in Christ. Piper says that you are being "stretched to the breaking point, the result is [greater faith and a] greater capacity to endure." Your faith is expanded and greater than it was when you were just enjoying the life before the storm. Press on for the greater faith.

* * *

http://solidjoys.desiringgod.org/en/devotionals/
suffering-that-strengthens-faith

194

BUILT ON THE ROCK

"Everyone then who hears these words of mine and does them will be like a wise man who built his house on the rock. And the rain fell, and the floods came, and the winds blew and beat on that house, but it did not fall, because it has been founded on the rock. And everyone who hears these words of mine and does not do them will be like a foolish man who built his house on the sand. And the rain fell, and the floods came, and the winds blew and beat against that house, and it fell, and great was the fall of it" ~Matthew 7:24–27

Jesus, ending His Sermon on the Mount with this parable, gives us an absolutely incredible visual of what we might build our lives on in this world. Both men in this parable are building homes. We'll look at the second man first.

The second man chooses a seaside home. It was gorgeous, right on the beach. The sun was always shining, and as they say in real estate, it was all about location, location, location. It's like one of those homes on Pacific Coast Highway in Malibu, right on the ocean. It's so close you can hear the ocean waves crashing from your bedroom. The beach house is the house where life is easy, good, and fun.

The first man built his home on the hill. It was more modest and had the basics: nothing extravagant, just useful and purposeful in its design. Building materials cost more, so the home was more humble, simple, and plain. It had quite a view of the ocean from the hillside but was more distant from the beach. Since it wasn't as accessible as the house on the beach, it took more effort and time to get to and held a greater cost and expense for guests who visited the house on the hill. Life was a bit more complicated there on the hill than on the beach.

What was each house built on? What are you building your life on? The man on the beach built his life in the most desirable location and was the envy of everybody. Everyone wanted to be his friend. He had the life everyone wanted. The man who built his home on the hill had a difficult time building his house up on that hill. It took a long time hauling the materials and digging the foundation. He wasn't overly envied, because it took so long to get to his house, and it was harder walking the steep paths to his house. The first man built on sand, had it all, and, for most people, was worth knowing because of what he possessed. The second man built on solid rock and had just that—a small house on a rock. It was harder to know the man up on the mountain. He didn't have a great house or great possessions. There was nothing materially that people received from knowing him.

No matter where a house is built, there will always be a storm that it is going to face. The storm these two builders faced may have been the same one, yet the outcome was completely different. The man who built his existence on the fun, carefree, excessive life at the beach found that his world had literally crumbled to pieces, been swept to sea, and could not be rebuilt. His life was completely destroyed because he built his life on the sand. It was soft, malleable, and changed with the slightest breeze. The man who built his house on the hill survived the storm. His house suffered damage, but his life was still whole; he could rebuild. He built his life on the rock, a solid foundation.

The reality of this passage is that the man who built his house on the rock built it on Jesus Christ; the other man built his life on the shifting sands of this world. You may be feeling that you built your life on things that aren't making life better for you—possessions, people, things that are as stable as the sand on the shore. The reality is that it's not too late to change foundations. Building your life on Christ is hard. It involves living for Christ instead of yourself. You can only survive this life through Christ, not through the things of this world or depending on people, your job, and your possessions. The man who built his life on the sand literally lost it all; there was no life left to live. It had been destroyed. The things he had built his life on failed him when the storm came.

The man on the hill, who built his life on Christ, his solid foundation, survived the storm. He lost much, like the first man, but not everything. He could rebuild his life because it was in Christ and was built for no other reason than for Christ alone. His foundation remained secure. Christ, as the foundation of your life, can help you endure any storm or trial life can throw at you.

PRAY ALWAYS

"Pray without ceasing" ~1 Thessalonians 5:17

Your trial has most likely brought you to your knees in prayer. You, as I do, may spend months, possibly years, on your knees, figuratively or literally, in prayer. Each hour, each day, each week may be spent in prayer for yourself, family, friends, doctors, upcoming appointments, procedures, finances, interviews, relationships, your workplace, or whatever is coming up in life.

As Paul wrote to the Thessalonians: "Pray without ceasing." My prayer is that you will follow the advice of Paul and spend every moment of your life bathed in prayer.

Prayer is simply you talking with God. It doesn't have to be anything fancy or formal. I have personally found such peace in merely talking with the Lord as I would with a friend. Prayer for the Christ-follower is exactly like the relationship Moses and the Lord had. "The Lord used to speak to Moses face to face, as a man speaks to his friend." (*Exodus 33:11*) God is not looking for flowery words. He is looking for a heart that desires to know Him, and prayer is a verbal expression of our hearts.

There were times when words could not express the depths of my heart, or times when I wanted to pray but just didn't know exactly what to say. I found the Psalms a wonderful way to pray when my own words failed me. They not only allowed me to communicate to the Savior in a way that honored Him, but I found that psalmists like David can relate so well to our current circumstances that each passage seemed to fit well.

The writers of the Psalms were blessed in writing their thoughts in a way that helped me through a drought of prayer, and they will help you also. Many times I had to ask myself, "How did David know exactly how I feel at this moment?" David didn't, but God did! Praying while reading the Psalms was an incredible blessing in my own suffering. I know it will be in yours.

Trials are common in this world, and the way through them is Christ—Christ alone. He longs to know your thoughts (positive and negative), your disappointments, your hopes, your dreams. He longs to know you, and prayer is one way that you and Christ grow closer together, and it is one more way that you can grow more like Him.

Pray like you have never prayed before. Christ is ready to listen, and He is there for you.

FIGHT OF FAITH

*"Fight the good fight of faith. Take hold of the eternal life to which you were called
and about which you made the good confession
in the presence of many witnesses" ~1 Timothy 6:12*

Your trial may be a fight for something: health, career, relationships,
possessions. But ultimately it is a fight for your faith. Trials are the
Olympic games of the Christian life. Your faith is on the line, and while
God is fighting for you and beside you, there is the obligation to fight
for your own faith too. God doesn't need you in this fight, because He
is more than capable of fighting for you on His own. The great truth
and pleasant reality is that He wants you fighting this fight, right beside
Him, as He fights on your behalf. Is there any greater ally than that?

Your faith is being tested in whatever your situation and wherever
you are in this life. You have a choice: give up or stay steadfast in the
strength of the Lord, which He's given you. There are way too many
who give up in the middle of the fight—even some believers.
Sometimes it feels too hard to continue on. Those who remain and stay
in the fight will exit their trial stronger, greater prepared for whatever
comes next in the pitfalls and ultimate joys of this life.

God will not abandon you in this fight. It's not in His character, and
He promises that He won't. He's in it until the end and then on into
eternity, where we will be with Him. Are you in this until the end?

ALL THINGS

"And we know that for those who love God all things work together for good, for those who are called according to his purpose" ~Romans 8:28

We have all heard this verse before and you may be hearing a lot of this in the midst of your storm. Hold on to the nugget of truth this verse brings, because in every way it will come to pass. God wants nothing but His greatest good for you. I know it's so hard during this journey to see any good now or even to think that any good can come. Yet, Paul's promise of how God works doesn't say "some things"; he says "all things." Let that set in: "All things work together for good." When all is said and done in your life, your struggles will result in good. You may find the trial will claim your life, that relationships might not be restored, or you might not get your dream job, but at the end of the day, it will "all work together for good." As a Christ-follower you know the next life; you know heaven. Is that not a good thing and a worthy goal? Is that not a promise for those who love God? Is heaven not the best thing that's going to happen in your existence, aside from salvation? Is not God's salvation the best thing you have ever received? I pray that you will hold on to the hope that your future in Christ is far better than the present struggles of your life.

Another truth is that things will work for your good "for those who are called according to His purpose." There are two truths in that statement: the truth of God's calling you in your salvation and the truth of God's calling you in your trial. Of the many calls the Lord can make of you, these two are the strongest and are placed on the hearts of all Christ-followers. Your life and your trial have purpose—a purpose unique to you and unlike any other. He has placed a call on your life, and all things will work for your good. The verse doesn't say that the trial is good, but it says the results will be good.

Endure to the end. It will be good—He promises!

BOOKENDS OF PSALM 139

"Even the darkness is not dark to you; the night is bright as the day, for darkness is as light with you" ~Psalm 139:12

If you have a few minutes, read through all of Psalm 139. If not now, read the psalm when you get a chance; it doesn't take that long. As you read, did anything stand out to you about the structure of Psalm 139? Below you'll find verses 1–3 and then verses 23–24:

Verses 1–3 say, *"O, L*ORD*, you have searched me and known me! You know when I sit down and when I rise up; you discern my thoughts from afar. You search out my path and my lying down and are acquainted with all my ways."*

Verses 23–24 say, *"Search me, O God, and know my heart! Try me and know my thoughts! And see if there be any grievous way in me, and lead me in the way everlasting."*

What is the connection between the two sections of this psalm? The connection is that God is searching the hearts of those who are faithful to Him, and David, the writer, welcomed God's search of his heart. These two passages from the psalm are not entirely about sin or purity in our lives. There certainly is an element of that, but even more so is the recognition, by the writer, that God knows every tiny detail of our lives. The God who is running the entire universe knows such simple things of our lives: when we lie down, when we rise, each breath that fills our lungs.

David was amazed by the works of God. Later, in verses 13 and 14, David writes: *"For you formed my inward parts; you knitted me together in my mother's womb. I praise you, for I am fearfully and wonderfully made. Wonderful are your works; my soul knows it very well."* David recognized God's intimacy in creation.

I don't know how popular knitting is, and I confess to not knowing the proper vocabulary, but think about someone sitting there, knitting a blanket. The knitter knows each thread; each stitch must pass through the knitter's hands before joining the overall creation. It's the same with

God: each part of your body, each day you will ever live, passed through His hands before coming into place in your life. God made you the way He did for a specific reason and purpose. Dear child of God, you truly are "fearfully and wonderfully made."

God can search you, because He knows you; every detail of your existence and life are within His hands. This may be an old illustration, but it is truly beautiful. Think of a tapestry. Someone has carefully crafted an image by using various colors of threads. But have you ever seen the back of a tapestry? It's just a mess of threads, and there is no semblance or organization at all. It looks chaotic; there is no order, and some even look like they are falling apart. The back of a tapestry is the view we have of our lives. We see the bits and pieces hanging loose from the fabric. It doesn't make sense; it's fractured; and it's confusing to try to figure out what's going on. During our lives all we see is the back of the tapestry. It might be that some of us see parts of the picture on the front side, but the truth is that we can never see the whole picture—at least not this side of heaven.

The Lord is working in your life, placing threads and bits and pieces to the fabric of your life. You don't see the final picture, because God is working on you from the moment you are born until the moment you die. It's only then, Christ-follower, that you will see the entire picture of the life that God has been working on since He formed you in the womb.

In knowing that God is searching our lives, David exhorted and encouraged us to seek God Himself, through His Word. God knows us intimately, but do we know Him intimately? Our current circumstances and trials are the perfect opportunity to see Him ever so clearly. God is not done with you; your picture is not yet completed. Your story is not yet finished.

THE TIMES THAT TRY MEN'S SOULS

"Many are the afflictions of the righteous;
but the LORD delivers him out of them all" ~Psalm 34:19

Trials have a way of refining us and getting rid of the trivialities and frivolities of our normal lives. It is almost as if our souls are tried and tested during our life's troubles, and truly they are. Every aspect of our lives is being tested. Thomas Paine, in 1776 (and I'm taking this completely out of context), wrote: "These are the times that try men's souls." You are in those times. Your entire existence is being tried: who you trust, your faith, your hope, everything about you. But like the refiner's fire, the goal is to come forth from the journey purer and stronger than before.

This trial is meant to strengthen your soul, not to weaken it or cause you defeat. Not only is your soul being tried in this, but those walking with you, those who are not, or those who are looking to see how you respond—who may choose to follow Christ because of you—are being tried and challenged as well.

When all is said and done, you will exit this trial stronger and purer than before. Your soul is being tried right now. The light of Christ will shine brighter through you because of it.

I CAN'T, BUT GOD CAN

*"But he said, 'What is impossible with men
is possible with God'" ~Luke 18:27*

God called my name in my cancer, and He is calling your name in your
present affliction, whatever it is you are facing. Part of His calling is so
we will call on Him wherever we are, whatever our situation. He wants
us to bend our knees in prayer and say, "I can't." I can't…sit through
this procedure, survive without a job, understand why my spouse left.
The "I cant's" of our lives are too numerous to count. He's calling us to
rest in His answer to the plea of our hearts, admitting that we can't. And
His answer is, "But I can."

The victory of your trial was won on the cross. It's not a victory
over physical death; it's a victory over eternal death—not being
separated from God forever but being with Him until the end of
eternity. You cannot save yourself from eternal destruction caused by
your sin. You can't go to God without Him first going to you. Someday
He will call you home to be with Him. Will you rest and trust in His plan
for every aspect—big or small—of your life?

What you can't do, God can!

FOR SUCH A TIME

*"And who knows whether you have not come to the kingdom
for such a time as this?" ~Esther 4:14*

One of the interesting things about the book of Esther is God's name is
never mentioned at all, nor does God seem to be the main character.
However, we see that God sometimes works behind the scenes in
mysterious ways to bring about His will. He was the main character in
Esther, just without the credit.

Esther was a Jewish orphan being raised by her uncle, Mordecai, a
scribe in the Persian king's palace. At the time there were many Jews
living in Persia, forced to leave after the fall of Israel many years prior.
The king, who dismissed his wife and queen for disobedience, longed
for another queen to take her place. He put out a call to all eligible
women to prepare, for over a year, for presentation to the king, after
which he would choose his new queen. After Esther was presented, the
king chose her as queen over Persia—without the knowledge that she
was Jewish.

An evil official, Haman, sought to annihilate the Jewish population
and deceived the king to agree to this genocide. Mordecai discovered
this plot and informed Esther of their impending doom. The king's law
said that absolutely no one might come before the king unsummoned,
facing death if they did. Esther had a choice: allow Haman to kill the
Jews or risk her own life to save them by approaching the king.
Mordecai reminded Esther that if she didn't tell the king about the plot,
God would bring help from someone else.

He asked her: "And who knows whether you have not come to the
kingdom for such a time as this?" God's call upon Esther's life was for
this very moment, to save or not save the Jews. She was given the
choice, but to deny the calling of the Lord would be a grave sin. The
Lord has made His own calling for your life, and for many of you, it's
currently this present darkness. To deny the Lord's work in your life is
sin. And depending on the purpose God has for you, He may find

someone else to fulfill His purpose if you don't allow Him to accomplish His purposes through you.

In many ways, your life has been saved for such a time as this, and like Esther, you may never know the long-term plan of God in your suffering. It may be the preservation of His people, someone's salvation, or some other glorious purpose. God's purpose in this trial is greater than you, and you do not always know the totality of His purposes and plan. God used Esther to save the entire Jewish population from extermination. Whether in great ways or small ways, God is using you and your trial.

Embrace God's purpose for you. It truly is greater than you could ever imagine.

TASTE AND SEE

"The LORD is near to the brokenhearted
and saves the crushed in spirit" ~Psalm 34:18

In Psalm 34, David wrote about God's deliverance, how blessed those
are who trust in God, and how the Lord hears the cry of His children. It
is worth reading and truly worth memorizing. Of all the verses in this
passage, one verse stands out, especially on this journey. It may seem in
this trial that sleep, taste, sight, and joy have all left you. And while all
those things may have left you, David reminds us in verse 8 that it's not
in this world we find those things, but in God.

"Oh, taste and see that the LORD is good! Blessed is the man who takes refuge
in Him!"

The Lord is taking us from the table of this world and seating us at
His table to look at how much better He is than anything this world may
hold and to show us how much stronger He is than anything we may
face.

In your trial He is forcing you to take refuge from the storms
around you and to do so in Him alone. I pray that you will find peace
and comfort in the refuge He has provided for you. There is a storm
raging around, but in the refuge of the Lord, all is well.

Taste and see the goodness of the Lord!

CAN'T BE SHAKEN

*"Therefore let us be grateful for receiving a kingdom
that cannot be shaken" ~Hebrews 12:28*

We don't know much about the kingdom of God except, as Christ-followers, we are already citizens of this kingdom. Jesus commanded us in Matthew: "Seek first the kingdom of God." (*Matthew 6:33a*) The command is given while we are still on the earth. From the moment of salvation we belong to that kingdom. But what kind of kingdom are we seeking? What kind of kingdom are we serving in?

The writer of Hebrews encourages us and gives us insight into this kingdom. It is a kingdom that cannot be shaken, ruled by an all-knowing God that cannot be shaken. As a citizen of heaven and servant of Christ, you too cannot be shaken. This is a kingdom that has always been in existence and always will be. Nothing can shake this kingdom; it is permanent beyond anything we know. Unlike the kingdoms and nations of this world, which will all fail and fall at some point, God will not fail and neither will His kingdom. You serve a God who cannot be moved and a kingdom that cannot be moved. Therefore, you cannot be moved.

Any plan God has for you cannot be thwarted, because even His plans cannot be shaken.

REFINER'S FIRE

"In this you rejoice, though now for a little while, if necessary,
you have been grieved by various trials, so that the tested genuineness of your faith—
more precious than gold that perishes though it is tested by fire—may be found to
result in praise and glory and honor at the revelation of Jesus Christ. Though you
have not seen him, you love him. Though you do not now see him, you believe in him
and rejoice with joy that is inexpressible and filled with glory, obtaining the outcome
of your faith, the salvation of your soul" ~1 Peter 1:6–9

It is not my desire to determine why you are in the midst of this trial. It would not be fair to say, as so many do, that it was caused by sin, or that God may think less of you than of other people. It may seem, as you look around at your peers, that some have been blessed beyond measure with "perfect" lives. Or maybe you are tempted to think that God delights in the suffering of some of His children. There is a reason and a purpose for the struggles of this life. Sometimes we find out that reason, but more often than not, we will never know.

The reality is that there is one purpose in any trial—to bring us closer to the Lord, by stripping the things of this world from our hearts and minds, and placing our hearts and minds completely on Christ. Our hearts are so entrenched in this world that many times our vision is blinded or clouded by the trappings of this world, even if those trappings are good (like relationships, prosperity, success, or family). Our trial is the refiner's fire to bring perspective and clarity on how to best live the life the Lord has laid before us.

The Lord desires the entirety of your heart, not the pieces that are not attached to this world, but your whole heart. You may kid yourself into thinking you have given God your whole heart, but how do you react when things are taken away? What thoughts go through your mind when you can't depend on your job, your health goes south, or people and relationships fail you?

You are being confronted in this trial with the priorities of your life. God is helping refocus your time and energy into what matters—Him and His kingdom. Don't resist the refiner's fire, but embrace God's purpose in growing you closer to Him and making you more like Christ.

In the end, I pray you will exit your trial closer to God, more Christlike, and stronger in the Lord than you were before.

SERVANTS OF OUR GOOD

"The LORD is my strength and my song, and he has become
my salvation; this is my God, and I will praise him, my father's God,
and I will exalt him" ~Exodus 15:2–3

God will turn our trials and sufferings into His, and our, joy. He is the conqueror and overcomer of our trials. We fight and participate in our struggle and turmoil, but it is He who does more fighting than we could ever do on our own. In actuality, He has already overcome every single trial we face in this life, including the greatest, our sin and death.

He can turn our deepest hurts into our greatest joys, but only through Him can that happen. We must allow Him to do His work in our lives to bring our greatest joy—Himself.

Someday you will look back, and there will be memories of the pain and hardship. But then there will be this joy that overcomes those emotions and memories. It is the joy God has given you in conquering, through His power, whatever it is you face.

DEFINITE PLAN OF GOD

"This Jesus, delivered up according to the definite plan
and foreknowledge of God" ~Acts 2:23

Before this world was created, God knew everything that would take place in all of history—all the billions who have lived, every breath and moment of our lives. God knew every second of each individual's time on this earth. He knew and planned your exact birthdate, your name, where you would live, and every decision you would ever make. He knew every word you would ever speak and every thought you would ever think. At the moment of creation, God had already been to the end of history and the beginning of your eternity with Him. He had experienced thousands of years of human history in the one instant before beginning it all. He had already written the story, with every minute detail, before putting anything in motion. There were no surprises for Him, and there never could be, because it is all His, under His complete control, at all times.

He knew mankind would fall into sin. He knew that every one of us would be sinners. However, He already knew His plan to save us would come through Christ, who knew before He came into the world the tortures and terrors He would face for your salvation. He knew everything, yet He still chose the cross, for your sake, for your salvation, so He could have a relationship with you. Jesus knew every single person who would accept His salvation and submit to His lordship over their lives.

Your trial, like all of history, is according to His perfect, definite plan. He knows your triumphs and your despairs, including every thought and every doubt you've ever had, or ever will have. God has planned this for your good and His glory. The most painful day in all of history, the crucifixion of Christ, was according to the plans of the Lord, made before the dawn of time. Look, Christ-follower, and see the goodness that has come from His death and resurrection in your life. Goodness will come from your painful experience. Like salvation, it will be a blessing to many.

WE KNOW YOUR NAME

"And those who know your name put their trust in you, for you, O LORD, have not forsaken those who seek you" ~Psalm 9:10

The Creator of the universe, the Lord, knows your name, and as a Christ-follower, you have the great privilege of knowing His name. There is great power in the name of the Lord, and He wants to work for your best interest at all times in your life. You have probably been in this trial for a while, and hopefully you have seen the name of the Lord upon your life and have put your trust in Him. In times of trouble, as you've seen, calling upon the Lord makes all the difference. His Spirit is within you, sealing you in your salvation and sanctification; He cannot and will not forsake you; He is committed to your greater good forever. Even if you do not seek Him, He is there. Remember, He sought you first in your salvation. God is ever faithful, even when He is quiet or when it seems like there is no hope.

The Lord never leaves those who know His name but works for their good until His energy is exhausted. And the question is: Will God's energy ever be exhausted? Will He ever stop working for your good? Never!

SOUGHT OUT

"But God shows his love for us in that while we were still sinners,
Christ died for us" ~Romans 5:8

God would be waiting for all eternity for anyone to come to Him. At no point would any of us of our own volition, or choosing, come to Christ for His salvation. Our sin is an example of us not going toward God but toward those things that displease Him, avoiding Him. That's why Christ came—to pursue us in our sin, to bring us salvation through Him and to have a relationship with His creation, you. The Lord is pursuing and prospering you in your trials, even if you don't see it or feel it. What better way to bring you closer to Him than through a relationship with God.

John Piper writes, "God does not wait for us to come to Him. He seeks us out, because it is His pleasure to do us good. God is not waiting for us; He is pursuing us." The Lord is actively pursuing us, even when we are not pursuing Him.

In trials God is doing us good, all for His glory. It gives Him delight to be at work in our lives and to bring about our ultimate good, even though there is much pain involved for us.

He is seeking and pursuing you in your dark valley. He is seeking your best in this, as hard as that truth might be to realize. Don't look on your circumstances as God punishing you. Trials are one way the Lord uses to rip our hearts from this world, and to place them in His hands so that we will trust in Him each step of the way.

Few people ever really get to see the strength of the Lord like you will during this time. That alone is a great gift and honor for you. He's not just seeking you, but He's fighting on your behalf. He's doing everything in His power for your good, right now.

Yes, it's hard, but there is such great blessing in having your heart solely focused on Christ—far more blessing than having the latest gadget, a big family, and a beautiful life. You have a beautiful Savior who is doing everything for you, and you get the immense joy of it just being Him and you on this path of greater glory. In the end, it will all be for your good.

* * *

http://solidjoys.desiringgod.org/en/devotionals/
how-much-god-wants-to-bless-you

NOTHING TOO BIG

"Behold, I am the LORD, the God of all flesh.
Is anything too hard for me?" ~Jeremiah 32:27

You and I both know we need a big God, not a small god, but don't you sometimes wonder, especially in the pain of life at the moment, if this is too big for God? Can He handle it? The doubt in your mind takes its toll on your weary soul. You've seen God work in so many ways, but it seems like, in your trial, that there isn't anyone who can handle the stress and weight of what you're experiencing. Take courage and realize that the Lord is big enough to handle anything that's thrown at Him, and at you. He's seen everything, experienced everything, and is intimately involved in your situation. You may not be able to handle your situation, but He can. Remember, He is God!

Can you think of a time when He failed you? Has He ever proven Himself unfaithful? Has the sun ever not risen in our world? There isn't one time when He has failed. His timing may be different from your expectations, but it's your expectations that are wrong, not His timing or response. He acts effortlessly in His perfect timing. The reality is, there may be no one on this earth who can handle what you're going through: no doctor, no employment recruiter, no counselor, no financial advisor, no friend. But God can! Just as He reassured Jeremiah of the strength of His might, He reassures you that He has everything under control, even when it seems like nothing is under control.

Nothing is too big or too small for God. If God chooses to, He will cure you, and even if He chooses not to, He is still God. He is God in the sun and God in the storm.

Think about this: creation was a mere walk in the park for Him, and right now, He's got you covered in His strength, love, and sovereignty.

HIS STEADFAST LOVE

"Give thanks to the LORD, for he is good,
for his steadfast love endures forever" ~Psalm 136:1

Psalm 136 is one of those psalms that you cannot read without taking something away—not that there are any psalms that do not touch our lives. No matter how well you memorize verses, a phrase from Psalm 136 will stay with you long after reading through it. The phrase is: "His steadfast love endures forever." The psalmist wrote on 26 different topics, events, and characteristics of the Lord. At the end of each topic, he wrote, "His steadfast love endures forever." It's not a mantra or incantation that you can repeat again and again and then something will happen, but it is a truth to hold on to during any part of life, and the psalmist wants us to know of God's steadfast love.

Whatever your trial is, whoever loves you or doesn't, remember that God loves you, and His love, His steadfast love for you, endures forever. When the psalmist writes *steadfast*, he means immoveable, permanent, unshakable; there is nothing that can change God's love for you. Truly His love endures forever. Through the ups and downs of your trial, and just in normal everyday life, His love endures.

Human love is so often fleeting, based on feelings or what you can get out of someone, but not God's love. His love for you is the same yesterday, today, tomorrow, and into forever. Your love for Him may waver during your trial, and He understands your plight, but believe this truth: His love does not and will not falter or fail. It cannot. It endures forever.

A BETTER COUNTRY

"But as it is, they desire a better country, that is, a heavenly one.
Therefore God is not ashamed to be called their God,
for He has prepared for them a city" ~Hebrews 11:16

As created beings, we certainly are frail in our humanity, with disease, financial problems, death, and sin plaguing our lives for all of our days. One day you will die, just as one day I will die. It's what comes after our passing from this world that we should be yearning for—a better country.

Hebrews 11 is known as the "Hall of Faith" for Christ-followers, containing examples of so many faithful Christians in perilous and unexpected situations who mightily demonstrated God's work and grace through their lives...and deaths. Every person on that list died on this earth, but each is so very much alive at this moment in heaven. They believed in Christ, despite situations that were far worse than most of us will face in this world (though I don't mean to minimize your situation at all). Those listed in Hebrews 11 saw beyond their circumstances, beyond this life, to see a better country. They saw what God had prepared for them and what He has prepared for you.

In the following quotation from J.R.R. Tolkien's *Return of the King*, Gandalf is talking to his friend, Pippin, as they face their imminent deaths, and about what comes after life. It fits so appropriately with our own struggle with mortality. Gandalf says,

> *"End? No, the journey doesn't end here. Death is just another path, one that we all must take. The grey rain curtain of this world rolls back and all turns to silver glass. And then you see it. White shores, and beyond, a far green country under a swift sunrise."*

Your life has a beginning and, amazingly, by the grace of God, has no ending. God has taken care of your passing from this life to the next. He is eager for you to join Him. However, the marvelous thing is, you cannot go until you have fulfilled God's calling and purpose for your life on this earth.

Isn't it exciting that God keeps you on this earth because He has a purpose for you?

Only when you've completed His work will you enter the better country.

IN EVERYTHING, GOD GLORIFIED

"Whoever serves, as one who serves by the strength that God supplies—in order that in everything God may be glorified through Jesus Christ. To Him belong glory and dominion forever and ever. Amen" ~1 Peter 4:11

As a Christ-follower, you are a servant of the Lord. God gives each of His children the strength to serve Him in whatever capacity He desires him or her to serve, whether in church ministry, vocation, missions, or wherever the Lord has placed that individual. He is giving you the strength to serve in your trial, because this is where He has placed you. Your trials are one of the greatest ministry and missionary opportunities you may ever have.

Peter showed you a purpose in serving the Lord in your ministry, especially in trials. The purpose was that "in everything God may be glorified through Jesus Christ." Christ is working in your life for His glory. He allowed this trial to happen, and He is directing your life each step of the way. Christ is in you, through the presence of the Spirit, and the Lord's ultimate goal is His glory. It has always been and always will be about His glory. Your life, my life, and the stories of our lives all boil down to this: God gets the glory. When you go to heaven and are in His presence, you will attest to all that He did in your life. Anything you might be able to boast of in this life is all given and directed by Him.

You see, nothing is ours; everything is His. "To him belong glory and dominion forever and ever. Amen."

TO EVERY SEASON

"For everything there is a season, and a time for every matter under heaven: a time to be born, and a time to die; a time to plant, and a time to pluck up what is planted; a time to kill, and a time to heal; a time to break down, and a time to build up; a time to weep, and a time to laugh; a time to mourn, and a time to dance; a time to cast away stones, and a time to gather stones together; a time to embrace, and a time to refrain from embracing; a time to seek, and a time to lose; a time to keep, and a time to cast away; a time to tear, and a time to sew; a time to keep silence, and a time to speak; a time to love; and a time to hate; a time for war, and a time for peace" ~Ecclesiastes 3:1–8

Could you read it without singing the '60s song by The Byrds? I never can read it without singing it in my head. While The Byrds may not have intended to sing about truth in trials, Solomon, the author of Ecclesiastes, did. He started the passage by saying, "For everything there is a season." Like all things in life, this trial is temporary; it is not forever. Enjoy the good times while they're here, because they will not always be present, and neither will the hard times always be there. Embrace the trials of this life and learn from them, never forget them, and remember them when things are good.

As God has decreed, so are the times of comfort and the times of hardship. In everything there is a season—the seasons of our lives. And just as the seasons of this world, this trial too shall pass.

FAR MORE ABUNDANTLY

"So that Christ may dwell in your hearts through faith—that you, being rooted and grounded in love, may have strength to comprehend with all the saints what is the breadth and length and height and depth, and to know the love of Christ that surpasses knowledge, that you may be filled with all the fullness of God" ~Ephesians 3:17–19

It is for Christ that Paul bows before the Father, recognizing the Father's infinite worth and power. It is in your current weakness that, hopefully, you too bow before the Father. You are doing as Paul did in Ephesians 3:14–21. You're taking a forced break from the stresses of each day and undertaking new stresses in these circumstances, but God is forcing you to bow before Him, to recognize His sovereignty, and to trust in His plan for your life.

In submitting to the Father, Paul got a glimpse of God's glory. As Americans we are so easily deceived by our material wealth—mere trinkets compared to the glory of the Lord. Paul reminded us to put our trust in the power of the Lord and not in the things of the earth.

As a Christ-follower you have the Spirit within you, "in your inner being." He is there, giving you the strength that you need to encounter every obstacle you meet along the way. The strength most likely will not be physical, but spiritual. Your body is fading away, but what you need most is Christ renewing the inner being of your soul.

During your trial, and at the end of your trial, you hopefully will have seen God work beyond anything you've ever seen. Paul wrote from personal experience that God can do "far more abundantly than all we can ask or think, according to the power at work within us." The Spirit is within you, believer, and God is going to act far beyond anything you could ever ask or think—beyond your wildest dreams. You won't see it in this life, but in the life to come. No doubt, God is acting on your behalf.

SHIELD ABOUT ME

"But you, O LORD, are a shield about me, my glory,
and the lifter of my head"~ Psalm 3:3

God stands in front of you, blocking and absorbing every blow that may come to you in this trial—not just some blows, but every blow from the attacker and accuser. No doubt this trial is painful, sometimes brining great physical or emotional pain. Christ takes so much more pain and hurt than you will ever feel.

Every fiery dart, sword blow, or flying bullet meant for you must first go through the Lord. It is not that He has a shield, but that He is *the* shield about you and your entire life. Yes, you feel the blows of the evil one, and it hurts. But God takes the full extent of each punch before it even reaches you. God is a shield about you in every way. He's the one protecting you in the storm and in the battle. He stands before you in your trial.

When David wrote that the Lord was a shield about him, he was saying that God was protecting his entire existence. Just as God protected David's existence, He is also protecting yours. He who is directing each step of your journey. Without Him you have no journey, good or bad. I am sure that there are days and weeks when the battle is fiercest and you can barely get out of bed, or even lift your head from the pillow. David says that God is "the lifter of my head," and so God will do that for you. When you don't have the strength to lift your head, to continue the fight, God is going to come alongside and lift your head for you. It is God who is going to give you the strength to fight on, to endure whatever each day may hold. He is fighting right beside you. He is going to motivate you to trust Him more each day, each step, and He is going to help make that happen for you.

Will you allow Him to be a shield about you?

A PLACE FOR YOU

"Let not your hearts be troubled. Believe in God; believe also in me. In my Father's house are many rooms. If it were not so, would I have told you that I go to prepare a place for you? And if I go and prepare a place for you, I will come again and will take you to myself, that where I am you may be also. And you know the way to where I am going" ~John 14:1–4

The reality is, at some point in this life we are going to physically die. It is a reality we don't like facing, but it's the truth. You may have faced someone's death in your trial, or you may be facing death yourself. It is strange to say, but in dying physically we find life, eternally, with Christ. Death certainly is scary; we don't know what it's like, because it's a path we have never taken, and can only take once. It's a path that's out of our control, because the Lord has numbered our days, not us. Yet there are many things to look forward to in the life to come, primarily being present with Christ.

Jesus, in John 14, was training His disciples, who like you and I, took a long time to train. They were discussing what came after this life, and Jesus assured them that the Father was preparing a place for Christ-followers. The reality is, God has a palace, and in this palace are many, many rooms—thousands, if not millions. And in this palace is a room that has your name on it. It's so strange—but so cool—to think that God has a place with each of our names on it. A place is already prepared for you in the life to come so that you may live it fully for His glory.

Death is hard. It requires leaving everything and everyone in this world behind, to travel the unknown road that all people must take. Look ahead and see that everything truly is in front of you, including the fullest life you could ever live.

Physical death is coming, but so is an eternity of life in Christ. To get one we have to do the other.

ONE PASSION

"Whoever loves father or mother more than me is not worthy of me, and whoever loves
son or daughter more than me is not worthy of me.
And whoever does not take his cross and follow me is not worthy of me.
Whoever finds his life will lose it,
and whoever loses his life for my sake will find it" ~Matthew 10:37–39

What is your one passion in this life? Your family? Your job? Your
financial security? Your friends? To one extent or another, our passions
detract and distract us from the greatest passion a person could ever
have, Jesus Christ. It's not that your passions are bad—many of them
are good—but without Christ your passions are nothing, and they mean
nothing. Christ must be your everything, the very passion and focus of
your life.

One of the amazing benefits that comes through trials is that our
passions are refocused to the end goal—that our passion becomes
Christ. Is Christ your passion? I pray that your current trial will increase
your passion for Christ.

In the end, as Christ-followers, we are spending eternity with Him.
Shouldn't we be really excited about Him? The things in this world
cannot hold a candle to knowing Christ. Though he didn't have good
theology, I pray that you will one day proclaim, as the German
eighteenth-century Christian leader Count Zinzendorf does, "I have one
passion. It is He and He alone."

Do you have that one passion in Christ?

AND YET WE GO

"And now, behold, I am going to Jerusalem, constrained by the Spirit, not knowing what will happen to me there, except that the Holy Spirit testifies to me in every city that imprisonment and afflictions await me. But I do not account my life of any value nor as precious to myself, if only I may finish my course and the ministry that I received from the Lord Jesus, to testify to the gospel of the grace of God" ~Acts 20:22–24

With the apostle Paul, it's easy to look at his life and think that he was a super-Christian, and in some cases he *was* farther along in his walk with Christ than many of us will ever be. But truly, Paul is no different than we are. He was a sinner, and Christ saved him. Like the trial you are currently in, Paul was in the midst of great trials in the book of Acts, especially toward the end of his ministry and the end of his time on this earth. Paul's perspectives on trials come only through Christ.

In Acts 20, Paul was preparing for his trip to Jerusalem. The Lord was prompting him to go there despite the various troubles that awaited him there. It was not an easy road for him, even though the Spirit was going with him. There were many fearsome obstacles ahead for Paul in going to Jerusalem, including many that could kill him. Paul admitted that he didn't know what was going to happen to him there. But he knew he wasn't going to be welcomed by most of the political and religious authorities. He knew his life may very well be on the line. Paul knew that there were afflictions wherever he went; there were a great number of people against Jesus Christ in the Roman Empire. And yet he still went anyway! He went where God called him, despite the risks to his own life.

Paul had an interesting perspective on life, the same perspective that I pray you are currently learning: Life without Christ has no value. Paul knew he faced the journey of his lifetime by going to Jerusalem. He knew that in the end it would cost him his life in Rome, but he didn't "count [his] life of any value." His life's desire was to finish what God had called him to do, proclaiming Christ wherever he went. The same calling is upon your life, and the reality for some is that Christ is calling for your life on this earth. Like Paul, you're going to spend and exhaust your life in ministry, giving yourself until there is nothing left, proclaiming the goodness of Christ to the last breath, and if not proclaiming in speech, proclaiming with each breath, action, and thought, that Christ is Lord.

Remember that your value is not in yourself, but in Christ and His beautiful claim and protection of your soul. It's a great reminder to finish the course of your life and the ministry that the Lord has set before you. You never know who you will meet, to whom you will minister to along the way, and who will be blessed by Christ through your life. This passage reminds us that we do not know where we are going on this journey, the troubles we will face, or how the path will end.

And yet we go, trusting Christ each step of the way.

MAGNIFY THE LORD

"Oh, magnify the LORD with me,
and let us exalt his name together!" ~Psalm 34:3

Psalm 34 is one of the most memorable psalms; demonstrating the worthiness of the Lord. The Lord is worthy of praise—in the light, in the dark, in the sun, and in the storm. No one said that it was going to be easy to praise God among the crashing waves, but it is the truth. Remember that you need to speak truth to yourself at all times, especially truth about God. He is your rock during this time, and whether life is great or you are struggling, God always deserves your praise. Giving praise to the Lord may be the hardest thing to do in your trial, but doing so is going to help you through your trial, to help you recognize and acknowledge His role and plan in your life. He is deserving of all the praise you can muster.

Let us praise Him together.

Will you magnify the Lord in your trial? Will you exalt and praise Him in these dark days?

NEED OF ENDURANCE

"For you have need of endurance, so that when you have done the will of God you may receive what is promised" ~Hebrews 10:36

Your trial may be short lived, or it may encompass many years. Either way, in your trial your strength is depleted. You have nowhere to turn, yet God is right there beside you through it all. It's hard to see God's will and purpose in this, and the reality is that you may never fully understand God's will in this trial. His will is beyond your complete understanding. In enduring your trial though—trusting in Christ and doing your best to live each day for His glory—you are doing the will of God. It is the Lord's will in this time of turmoil for you to rest in Him, to take your eyes off the things of this world, and to fixate your heart on Christ.

The end of the trial may be a day, two days, a month, a year, or even decades away, but it will end. God has promised that. What is it that God promises in the passage above? The promise is Himself. You get this rare opportunity in your trial—which so many believers throw away—to get to know and see your Savior in a new light. It's not that you didn't see Him before, but you get to see Him clearer and purer than before, untainted by the distractions of this world.

At the end of the book of Job, everything and more is restored to him. Unlike Job you may not have restored to you all that you have lost. You may continue to struggle financially for many years to come, or your health may continue to fail; God makes no promises to that end. He promises Himself to you. That is far better than any wealth, relationship, job, or health you may have in this life. Your relationship with Christ is to grow stronger and deeper over time until you begin your eternal life with Him—without suffering, tears, or pain. He promises Himself, and that should be enough to help you endure whatever storms you are in the middle of. Can you trust that Christ is enough?

GAIN YOUR LIFE

"By your endurance you will gain your lives" ~Luke 21:19

The end times will be a very scary time in which to live. The world will literally be falling apart, all to herald Christ's glorious return. There will be no time in human history as hard as that future time period. The world will be rocked by wars, calamities, and trials of the greatest magnitude for all who are still living. There will be Christ-followers who will face these times, and there will be trials beyond comparison and understanding at the end. He gives hope to those who will live during this time, and He gives hope to you in the calamities of your own life.

He says, "By your endurance you will gain your lives."

Where does this endurance come from? Is it within us? The reality is that many will admit to not having the strength to awaken each morning during their trial. Even though people may say to us how strong we are during this time, you and I know that it's not a strength that we possess; it's the strength of Jesus. It's difficult, and it's okay to say we're weak. Why? Because in our weakness God gets the best opportunity to show us His strength. God can use you more in your weakness than He can in your strength.

Enduring to the end, whether to the end of the trial or the end of our lives, yields what? At the end of our trial we are closer to Christ than when we entered the trial. At the end of this life we get to be with Christ.

Endure, my friend, to the end, and Christ will be there in all His glory.

HOME IS NOT HERE

"For here we have no lasting city,
but we seek the city that is to come" ~Hebrews 13:14

Take a look around. Your family, friends, colleagues, acquaintances, and random people on the street are all doing the same thing—building and making their homes here. We spend thousands of hours and dollars buying, building, outfitting homes, cars, and clothing, among thousands of materialistic things we pursue. It's as if we are building memorials to ourselves, and the reality is that none of it will last. To be honest, these aren't bad things, but sometimes they distract from the reality of our mortality, and the future that we have beyond this world.

This may come as a surprise to you, but this world is not your home. You are not a permanent resident of this world. The time and money you spend on your own comforts is, in many ways, a waste, because it's not permanent. You may already have realized that if you've lost your home, job, or the material comforts of the American dream.

As a Christ-follower, your home, your country, your entire existence is with and in Christ. You are just a transient resident in this world, waiting to pass into His glorious presence. Recognizing this reality puts everything into perspective. In the end, what truly matters is Jesus, not the life you've built here or the life you hold on to so very desperately.

A colleague of mine told me at the start of the school year that none of us is irreplaceable, and that is a truth that each of us needs to take hold of and dwell on. In terms of a job, there will always be someone who is able to take your place—maybe even someone who would be a better employee and do a better job. At some point, someone else is going to live in your house, and yes, they'll change it in ways you never intended. There is always someone better out there. There is no better God, though, than the One you serve—not one.

Your future on this earth may be very painful, very empty in terms of comforts, but your best life is not now, it never is, it never has been, it was never intended to be, and it never will be. Your future lies not in

232

this world but across the horizon into eternity. Whatever future the Lord has for you on this earth, however painful and distressing or happy and prosperous, your best days are always ahead. Your best life is yet to come, and no matter how desperate your situation gets, there is always hope in what's coming, and you can face anything because of the promises Christ has given to you in His Word.

You are His and are cherished by Him, and He is fighting for you in every part of this dark trial. The best life is being in His presence, not in the wealth and comfort you amass on earth. Christ is your home, not the world. When you cross over into the great beyond, each day is going to seem more astonishing and astounding than the day before in the kingdom of the Lord.

Are you building your best life in this world, or are you building for your upcoming life in heaven?

WALK THROUGH FIRE

"When you pass through the waters, I will be with you; and through the rivers, they shall not overwhelm you; when you walk through fire you shall not be burned, and the flame shall not consume you. For I am the LORD your God, the Holy One of Israel, your Savior" ~Isaiah 43:2–3

God knows the hardships you face and is sympathetic to your plight. He knows there are rough times ahead. Thankfully, He doesn't paint over or façade that fact. In Christ, you will have hard times. But He doesn't leave you alone in these times. No, not at all. He says there will be tidal waves, roaring rivers, and a crucible of fire. You are in the midst of treading water and just surviving, but God hasn't just sent you into the trial to sink or swim. He's planned this for you since before you were born, and He will be there in your trial until the end.

He tells Isaiah, and us, that it is He who allows our trial to occur, but it is also He and, only He, who is our Savior.

Rest in the great peace of mind given to us through Isaiah.

CONCERNING ABRAHAM

"No distrust made him waver concerning the promise of God, but he grew strong in his faith as he gave glory to God, fully convinced that God was able to do what He had promised" ~Romans 4:20–21

Have you ever been forced to move from your home not knowing where you were to live? The Lord required this of Abraham: to leave his home and venture to a land he had no knowledge or experience with. Have you ever been asked to sacrifice something great, like a child? The Lord required Abraham's son to be sacrificed. Have you ever been promised something that you know will come true, but you knew that you would never see it fulfilled? The Lord made Abraham the promise of having descendants that outnumbered the stars.

Like Abraham, God is requiring certain things from you, primarily your life. It's not written in the scriptures, but I am sure Abraham had some doubts about God's plan. The Lord asked him to leave everything he knew and move to a foreign land. The Lord promised Abraham and his wife a child, far after their childbearing years had passed. God fulfilled His promise in their son, Isaac. When God had fulfilled the promise of a son, the Lord then asked for Isaac to be sacrificed. Abraham trusted God, even if it meant giving Isaac to the Lord.

The Lord promised Abraham that every single person who would ever live in the entire world would be blessed by him, but Abraham would never live to see the promise answered. Doesn't just one of those things that God asked or said to Abraham require a lifetime of trust?

In the Romans 4, Paul writes about Abraham, well over a thousand years after Abraham lived, to tell readers that God was still presently fulfilling the promises God made to Abraham. He knew that challenges lay ahead in trusting God and His promises. As he struggled with what God required of him, Abraham believed that God was going to be faithful to the promises He had made. Abraham's faith was tested beyond what most of us could bear. Yet, when tested, Abraham grew strong.

The Lord took Abraham's faith to the breaking point, and it was God who strengthened Abraham's faith, to the glory of God. Abraham knew and trusted that if God made a promise, He was going to make good on that promise.

God will do what He promises. He guarantees it. After all these years, the promise of God to Abraham—blessing the world through Abraham—is still coming true. As a Christ-follower you are an example of God fulfilling this promise, because you are a member of Abraham's family. You are represented by one of the stars Abraham beheld as he looked in the sky as God made His promise. Isn't it amazing to be a part of God's great promises? God's promises may not be as extensive to you as they were to Abraham, and just like Abraham, you may never fully see the full extent of God's work in and through your life while you live. But you will see it someday. There is no better way to end than with Paul's words: "So then, those who are of faith are blessed along with Abraham, the man of faith." (*Galatians 3:9*)

As Abraham was blessed by the Lord, so will you be blessed, maybe not this side of heaven, but there is so much life to be had in the life to come. Will you trust the Lord as Abraham did?

ACKNOWLEDGE HIM

"Trust in the LORD with all your heart, and do not lean on your own understanding.
In all your ways acknowledge him
and he will make straight your paths" ~Proverbs 3:5–6

If you've been in the church for any amount of time you're very familiar with this passage from Proverbs. I hate to say that it is one of those verses that may have been worn out from being quoted too often, but it is one of those verses that *can* bring great comfort if we focus on its meaning and intent. Let's look beyond the surface to see how we can grow.

No doubt you are trusting in God, but are you trusting in Him with your whole heart? He wants you in your entirety, to the depths of your heart, not pieces of your life. He wants your whole soul and entire existence, not just part of your life. He wants you to trust Him with all you've got, every ounce of energy in your storehouse, the entirety of your existence. He doesn't want part of you, but all of you.

People have most likely given you advice in your situation. They may mean well, but don't let their words distract you from God and His Word. Your own knowledge and understanding can so easily betray you in these times when you may not be thinking clearly. Even in the times when you think clearly you can deceive yourself. Wrong thinking leads to wrong decisions; right thinking, grounded in the Lord, leads to strength and growth in Christ, especially in having a true view of God's sovereignty over your life.

Prayer is a way for you to acknowledge the Lord in every step and in every part of your journey. No doubt you clearly play a big role in your story, but God plays an even bigger one. Acknowledging His work in your life is a way of bringing praise to Him. It is also a witness to His work in your life, for others to learn from, in hopes that they too may be saved. Each day is a new opportunity for the Lord to direct and straighten your path in this life and to make it clearer. He knows you;

He knew you before you were born, and He knows exactly where He is taking you on this journey. Each step of your life is directed by Him, according to His will and ultimate purpose.

Walking with God and trusting Him and His sovereignty may be the greatest joy you'll find in this suffering.

WALK BEFORE THE LORD

"The LORD preserves the simple;
when I was brought low, he saved me" ~Psalm 116:6

The Psalms are such a beautiful gift from the Lord to His children at any stage of life, in any mountaintop or valley. They are absolutely remarkable. Take a moment and read through Psalm 116.

All over this earth, all around this life, you and I, and all of humanity, are living in the land of the dying. The reality is that every single person on this earth will physically die someday. But on this earth right now, all around us, people are dying spiritually. Death is all around.

However, as a Christ-follower, you are in the land of the living. Each day you live, you are heading toward physical death, but each day you live you are gaining more and more life in your soul through Christ. You are growing stronger, more Christlike, with each day.

It's hard to think in this trial that you are in the land of the living. When I was in the ICU after each of my two surgeries, I did not feel like I was in the land of the living. I was segregated from the other patients, who were sedated and hooked up to more machines than I was. Some of them would die while I was in the hospital. Physically I was in the land of the dying. You may feel the same way every time you're waiting in the doctor's office or in line at the DMV. However, I can say that while being awake at 2:00 a.m. in the ICU, I was never more alive, and my life was growing stronger because of Christ.

Verse 9 of Psalm 116 says, "I will walk before the LORD in the land of the living." Christ-follower, you may be dying, depressed, or paralyzed by fear, but that's just it; as a Christ-follower you are in the land of the living, walking with the Lord. The Lord goes with you wherever you go, wherever you are. He knows the land through which He's taking you. Sin brought suffering and death in this world; God brings life. Only in Christ can you have eternal life.

At the end of the day, when the trial is over and you're out of the valley, I pray that you will say with the psalmist, the Lord has "dealt bountifully" with you.

DON'T LET IT FALL

"And Jesus said to him, 'If you can! All things are possible for one who believes.'
Immediately the father of the child cried out and said,
'I believe; help my unbelief'" ~Mark 9:23–24

Our faith in Christ is extraordinary. It comes from the Lord, and as Christ-followers it's a part of you—a part of your identity and actions. At times you have seen your faith tested and tried, and at times you've seen your faith blessed on this journey. You have felt at times like the father in Mark 9: "I believe; help my unbelief." John Piper exclaims in his article on God's giving us faith: "Let us pray daily! O thank you for my faith. Sustain it. Strengthen it. Deepen it. Don't let it fail. Make it the power of my life, so that in everything I do, you get the glory as the great Giver. Amen!"

Pray each day for your faith, and like Piper, pray that the Lord will sustain you, strengthen you, deepen you, and not allow your faith to fail. At times on this journey you may have nothing to hold on to except for your faith. His promise to you is that in Him, your faith cannot fail.

* * *

http://www.desiringgod.org/articles/
god-has-allotted-to-each-a-measure-of-faith

THE DAY IS AT HAND

"The night is far gone; the day is at hand" ~Romans 13:12

No doubt you have seen some very dark days, and darker days may be ahead. No doubt the sun is probably not shining as brightly in your life right now as it did before your trial. The reality is you already have the sun, the Son of God, shining brilliantly in the midst of your darkest night. It doesn't mean that His presence will take away the darkness of the valley, but it does mean His light will shine in such a way to guide your steps and lead you into right thinking.

In all of human history dawn has always come, and the sun has always risen. It has always arrived each morning in its own glorious light, all under the direction and command of the Lord. There has never been a single day in the history of the world when the sun hasn't risen in the morning in all its brightness.

The sun, too, will shine again in your life; your trial will pass. It may be a day, a month, a year, or even a lifetime before it shines again. Yet in death, you will pass into the glorious light and life the Lord has prepared for you and for all Christ-followers. Night can only exist for a short time; the day will come.

As Victor Hugo wrote in *Les Miserables:* "Even the darkest night will end, and the sun will rise."

And all that, by the hand of God.

DEATH OF HIS SAINTS

*"Precious in the sight of the LORD
is the death of His saints"* ~Psalm 116:15

Don't you find this verse a bit odd? God is saying that death is precious to Him—the death of His saints no less, not His foes or enemies, but His saints.

Sin has caused a great split in our relationship with God. Sin separates us from God because of His holiness. Jesus was sent to bridge the gap caused by our rebellion, our selfish nature, and our sin. Even as Christ-followers we are physically separated, because sin still exists in our world. The Lord desires a relationship with His creation. Yet all seven billion of us are sinners and separated from Him because of our sin.

This verse still doesn't make sense. It is perplexing that God would delight in our death. But there are a couple of facets to this verse. The first is, our goals, intentions, and dreams die so that God becomes our greatest desire in this life. The second is even more profound: God wants you in His presence. Only in your death can He physically be with you, hold you, embrace you. His longing to see you far outweighs any trials He may allow in this life to bring you closer to Him.

But He has a job for you to do on this earth, and while you are completing that job in His strength and power, He is preparing a place for you in His presence. Because you and God have never seen each other face to face, He really is excited about the future. He longs to develop an even deeper relationship with you when you are physically present with Him.

SCARS – YOUR STORY, GOD'S GLORY

"See my hands and my feet, that it is I myself. Touch me, and see. For a spirit does not have flesh and bones as you see that I have" ~Luke 24:39

Men love talking about their scars; women, probably not so much. Men talk about the adventures and experiences in which they "earned" their scars. The bigger the scar, the cooler the story, the better the man. It's one of the many ways men determine who's the best and the baddest.

Trials and the journey of suffering you're on will leave a scar, whether physically, emotionally, or both. Trials have a way of changing your life more than you think. The scars tell your personal story: what you went through, how you stayed strong, and what you learned or will learn. Your scars also tell God's story. Remember, God is gloriously at work in your life during trials. Your scars direct your story to His story and are a way for you to talk with others about how God brought you through your trial. It's an opening for you to display God's story before others who are in a trial, in hopes they may be exhorted in Christ or come to salvation.

Scars don't just tell a story, they also show signs of healing and growth. They show that something was at work beyond your control, that someone was working behind the scenes. Healing may take a while, but thankfully the Lord will direct it, and your scar and story will also be His scar and story. The scars will always be there, and the trial is leaving its mark on your life—in many cases for the rest of your life—but it shows that you've come through something significant and have survived to tell about it.

Don't hide your scars. Use them as a testimony of the hand of the Lord upon your life!

TO LIVE

"For to me to live is Christ, and to die is gain" ~Philippians 1:21

You and I have learned that our days are numbered. Some of us have a pretty good guess of how many days or years we have, but most have no idea how many we have—except we think we will live to a ripe old age. The reality is, few of us truly think about the life we are living and whether we are truly living life to the fullest. I'm not talking about the experiences we have, the weak relationships, or any of the shallow things of this life. We have to ask ourselves if we are truly living. As Christ-followers, are our lives really being lived for Christ? Are our relationships deep and abiding? Are we proclaiming Christ to all we meet?

My prayer is that this trial will energize you to live this life with all your might, right until the end—to live in the strength of the Lord, while you live, for as long as the Lord allows.

As a young man in the eighteenth century, Jonathan Edwards created a list of resolutions by which to live and arrange his life before the throne of God. While he made them personally for his own steadfastness as a Christ-follower, the truth of many of his resolutions fit our current walk with Christ and our current trials.

Can you commit to the second of Edwards's Resolutions, "To live with all my might, while I live"?

TO THE END

"Now faith is the assurance of things hoped for,
the conviction of things not seen" ~Hebrews 11:1

Your faith is on trial. Will it survive and endure to the end, or will it falter and fail? You have a great many brothers and sisters who, in trials far worse than yours, endured to the end of their trial or their life. Their faith was tested, and in the grace of God, they remained faithful to the end.

Hebrews 11 records these amazing people of faith. Read through it. Some of the names are familiar, yet many names are not even listed, especially in verses 32 through 40. These are people to whom God promised something. They believed and pursued the Lord, and in the end they never saw God's promises to them fulfilled. The most amazing thing is that while they never saw the complete fulfillment of God's promises, they still believed. Abraham never saw the Promised Land; he never saw his descendants be as numerous as the stars or the promise of Messiah fulfilled in Jesus Christ, yet he continued on in his faith.

Christ-follower, there are so many people who have gone before you as examples of walking by faith, when your eyes may not see the end goal in your own sufferings and life. At the end of Hebrews 11, there are many named who died horrific deaths, yet their faith never wavered. Until the end they proclaimed the salvation of Christ. They trusted that what God had promised would come to pass, whether they saw it or not. It wasn't the fulfillment of the promise that stirred their faith; it was that God had made them a promise, and they rested in the fact that God would fulfill all of His promises.

Will you trust in the Lord to whatever end He has for you?

AS WE PART

This journey will take you to unimaginable places: to the highest of heights and, most likely, to the deepest of depths. I have prayed for you every day while writing this, and while we may not know each other personally, my prayer has been that during your trial you will see God as He is—not merely as you want Him to be. My prayer is that you are trusting in God with every breath that you have, allowing Him to work in your life. I pray that the church is beside you in your struggle, lifting you in prayer and providing for your needs both physically and spiritually.

Father,

> In Your plans, purposes, and wisdom, You selected and called each of us to a spectacular journey. Your desire since the dawn of time has been to have a relationship with us and a restored relationship with Your creation. We know that You have selected us for Your kingdom, and in our present darkness we are struggling. We are struggling to see Your hand at work, struggling to see the purpose of our suffering. Yet, O Lord, we know there is such glorious purpose in Your plan for our journey.

> We trust in You, as Sovereign God, that You are working in our lives to bring us great light in the darkness, to deliver us, and yet to also stretch our faith, to expand Your kingdom, and to see Your hand and will at work in our lives. We pray for the faith and strength to press on and persevere in this life, knowing the future life You have secured for us, Your children, in Your kingdom. We pray for humility, peace, and contentment that only You can give. Help us to walk in truth and love as we embrace Your plan for our lives. To

You, O Lord, do we commit the entirety of our lives and souls to use for a purpose far greater than ourselves. We place our lives into Your hands, knowing that in Your wisdom, and through Your purposes, You will direct each moment of our lives. At times we will not know where You are taking us, but we are grateful that You know. We find the days dark and burdensome, the future full of uncertainty, but the days are bright and the future hopeful with You. Your Word is a rock for us to look to in these times.

Into Your hands, Lord, we place our entire being and existence, to work as You see fit. May we be willing vessels of Your will. Amen!

FACEBOOK TESTIMONIES

The following entries are my personal testimony that I shared with others on Facebook (I know, I know I still use Facebook) as I journeyed through cancer, and one from 2015, the year of recovery. They were written in the midst of the trial. They appear here exactly as they did on Facebook. I did not edit them, because I want you to see how God worked in my life and how I used my situation to enrich others' lives. I do not want to draw your attention to my situation but want to draw you to God through my situation.

Testimony Facebook Post 1

In the midst of the storm on the Sea of Galilee, the disciples worried. They worried about their lives, their livelihood, and their families. All seemed lost. And yet, in the storm, Jesus slept. It was not that Jesus was indifferent to the storm or the needs of the disciples, but there is nothing that surprises God. Jesus is God! And in His perfect timing He acted to calm the storm, to calm the sea, to act on His promise to never leave or forsake those who are His, those who belong to Him, those who have trusted in Him as their Lord and Savior.

Neither will He leave or forsake us in the many storms we may face in life, however great or small. Jesus is right there. There is nothing that surprises Him because He already knows the outcome, the answers. He may seem quiet or absent, but He is right there, waiting for His perfect timing to act. And He will act, sometimes in ways we don't want, but remember He is God, and His ways are far beyond and far better than ours.

As my pastor, Todd Smith has quoted, originally from J. Vernon McGee, "This is God's universe and He does things His way. Now, you may have a better way of doing things, but you don't have a universe."

Testimony Facebook Post 2

So I had Lord of the Rings on last week at the house and a quote stood out to me about life. I'll quote it as best as I can remember. Frodo says to Gandalf, "I wish none of this had ever happened." There are so many things in our lives that we never wished had happened, whether big or small. Yet I was reminded that there is reason and purpose in the trial the Lord has placed in my life. Over the past six weeks I've learned that nothing happens by coincidence and everything, including every conversation I've had, has purpose in it.

Returning to the quote, Gandalf says in reply, "So do all who live to see such times. But that is not for them to decide. All we have to decide is what to do with the time that is given us." God has given each of us a certain number of days, just as He has given us so many hairs on our head. Sometimes we're blessed to know when our time is up and sometimes we don't. However, our days are already determined for us. Our role lies in making the most of our days. I've learned that our role is to change lives, not to direct people to look at us, but to direct them to look at Jesus, to show His glory to people who are striving to know Him. I guess you could say the decision is already made for us on what we do with our days.

Tomorrow I take a step I never thought I would take. It's not in my hands, but in the Lord's. Am I scared? Yes, who wouldn't be? Do I know the entirety of the path I'm on? No, but God does. And the amazing reality is that, as the picture shows, God already does. I know a small amount of what's going to happen tomorrow, but God knows it all. I am choosing to lift it up to Him, to lay it at His feet because He's already there. And He's there the next day, the day after that, and the day after that. There certainly are emotions and if I exhibit any strength it doesn't come from me, but we serve a big God who has given each of us a role, a purpose, just as each situation we find ourselves in has a role, a purpose. Our lives are truly greater than ourselves.

Testimony Facebook Post 3

Today I gladly part ways with my enemy and foe, my brain tumor. To do so I will undergo what they call an occipital craniotomy resection of tumor, or in layman's terms they'll cut into my scalp and skull, dig through [three inches of the brain] and remove the tumor, [return my skull to its proper place, screw it in,] and then staple it all closed. And if I'm lucky I'll get a great tattoo, all while asleep!

This is the hardest part physically of this cancer journey so far. At the end of the day, it doesn't mean I'm cancer free, but it does mean the closing of one chapter and the opening of a new one. Brain cancer has forever changed my life and tomorrow when I awake in the ICU I will start a new normal, a new way of living life, all with a new perspective and outlook on life itself. And thanks be to the Lord for this!

However, in this new chapter I'm not letting cancer define me. The only definition I have for my life is in Christ. I learned early on in this journey that this is more of a spiritual than a physical journey. I only asked God the question, "Why me?" once and [quickly came] to ask, "Why not me?" instead. As people we tend to place things in good columns and bad columns, and certainly cancer is bad, physically that is. But I have seen so much good in this journey so far and the joy of this road far outweighs the physical battle that is and is yet to be. God has great purpose in this. While I don't know [yet] the full extent of His purpose, I will say I've seen things and learned things that I would not have learned any other way than through this journey of cancer. I've seen God work in ways indescribable, in my life and in the lives so many who are walking this journey with me. I've grown so much closer to my Lord and Savior Jesus Christ. It has been my hope and prayer that in this journey we all would see Christ, and Him glorified.

One of the greatest lessons I have learned is how big God is. I'm reminded that if God knows the number of hairs on my head, He most certainly can direct each cell in my body to do His will. He told Moses in Exodus, "Who has made man's mouth? Who makes him mute, or deaf, or seeing, or blind? Is it not I, the Lord?" (Exodus 4:11). Nothing is outside his control and more than anyone or anything, He can use the bad in this world for His great glory. This cancer and the many trials of our lives are within His grasp and nothing happens without His direction or allowance.

My life belongs to Christ. I have submitted to Him and laid everything at His feet, my hopes, my dreams, my life, and this cancer. His plans are far better than mine and as few of my expectations in this life have ever come to pass, I rest in the truth that Christ is in control. He only does what is good for His children. He can take the heartaches and trials of this life and turn them into precious truth for His glory, and in that it is a great life! [It is] a great honor and privilege to be used as a part of His mighty plan.

In the end this isn't just my journey. Yes, I've had the physical aspect of this journey, but this is your journey too. There is something for you to learn, to be challenged in some aspect, to know and grow closer to Jesus. And I know at the end of this journey I'll be with Christ for all eternity, seeing an end to the sorrows of this world and embracing my Lord, my Savior. As I go into surgery today, I leave you with this, Romans 8: 37-38: "No, in all these things we are more than conquerors through him who loved us. For I am sure that neither death nor life, nor angels nor rulers, nor things present nor things to come, nor powers, nor height nor depth, nor anything else in all creation, will be able to separate us from the love of God in Christ Jesus our Lord."

Testimony Facebook Post 4

Thank you all for the outpouring of love and support. I have never felt the goodness of Christ more in my life [than] the past few months and how the Lord has answered prayers beyond my belief. My brain surgery went very well and the doctor feels he got most of, if not the entire tumor, with a good margin. I will find out the final neuropathology report in about a week and then we can discuss treatment options, if any. I went home from the hospital on Friday and while recovery is a bit slower than my biopsy in June and my vision is slowly improving, I can expect to make a full recovery within a few weeks to months. Once again I have to look to the Lord and point to Him and His grace in this. We will all face trials that are sometimes beyond belief in our lives—like this diagnosis of brain cancer has been for me and my family—and it's what we do with them that makes all the difference. Whatever trial you may face in this life, big or small, know that Jesus is there right beside you. Reach out your hand to Him and He will grab a hold of it and never let go. All you need to do is reach [out] and He'll hold on and do the rest. It doesn't mean you're not going to cry, or get angry, or not understand what's going on, but trusting in the One who does makes it all the easier.

As I mentioned in another post, this road is not over, but is now taking a new direction. While I haven't read your many messages and comments (it's kind of hard right now) I hope to over the next few weeks and dare I say months. But please know I appreciate the support and love. It's made this journey all the more easier. Thank you!

Testimony Facebook Post 5

The past two Sundays my pastor has talked about Open and Closed Doors. While specifically related to the missionary journey of Paul and Silas in the book of Acts, we have so many open and closed doors in our lives, as Jesus directs us into and through His will. There is only one door open in my life at the moment and with Christ, I'm boldly walking through it.

I haven't given an update in some months. Two weeks ago I received my final diagnosis and statistical prognosis from UCLA. I was diagnosed with anaplastic astrocytoma grade III cancer [later changed to anaplastic ependymoma grade III]. It is a primary brain cancer of which there is no cure, just monitoring and maintaining my current progress. Most likely this will return in 5-10 years and can return as a higher-grade cancer. This next week I will start six weeks of daily radiation and a year of a chemotherapy pill. There is now this shadow of cancer over the course of my life, but the light of Christ overshadows that. Thankfully my most recent MRI, two and a half months after surgery and without any treatment, shows good healing, little scarring, and most important, no regrowth of the cancer.

As I left UCLA that day two weeks ago, I was reminded of Psalm 90:12, "So teach us to number our days that we may get a heart of wisdom." It's absolutely amazing to see the truth of scripture come alive in my life. The Lord has placed a certain number of days upon our lives; some of us have a greater number of days and some of us a lesser number. Some of us Christ-followers are walking more quickly toward heaven, and some of us more slowly. It's not the number of days that matter but the quality of our days, the quality of the time the Lord has given to us on this earth.

There are many things I expected for my life, such as the picture perfect picket fence family, with a smokin' hot, loving wife and brood of little Hollands running around, living until I was 95 and quietly falling asleep and never waking up. The Lord has directed my days and steps to where so many things I expected or wished have not come to pass yet. I never imagined being a teacher, yet I absolutely love it and have seen lives change before my eyes. I confess that so many trivialities, frivolities and vain pursuits no longer matter. The perspective and focus of my life has completely changed, and all for the better.

I enter through the only open door right now I have, with no expectations other than this, to see Jesus act in accordance with His will for the sake and glory of His kingdom, of which I'm so grateful to be a part of. As hard as this life trial has been, it's been a joy to be gifted with the perspective that my life has a time limit, an expiration date. If one person is changed because of this trial, beyond myself, and one person can see the hand of God in this and trust Jesus as their Lord and Savior, then any pain of this life has been absolutely worth it. Whether I eat or drink, live or die, I stand as a son and follower of Jesus Christ and to Him I owe my life and the blessings and trials therein. What a joy it is! And I can only pray that what Paul says in 2 Timothy 4:6-8, is also true of me, and in the long life ahead. "The time of my departure has come. I have fought the good fight. I have finished the race, I have kept the faith. Henceforth, there is laid up for me the crown of righteousness." And at the end of my days I can only pray to hear Jesus say to me, "Well done, good and faithful servant (Matthew 25:21)." There is a lot of fighting ahead both physically and spiritually, but I'm going to fight! My story is not over and neither is yours! (By the way, I'm not dying, just fighting to live! I feel great and am ready for whatever each day holds! Hopefully a good nap!)

Testimony Facebook Post 6

A year ago today, I sat with my family in a cold doctor's office awaiting results I did not expect. I found out about the brain tumor the week prior, and felt naively that we could handle that, but was entirely unprepared for the doctor to say it was cancer.

The world stopped for me at that moment and truly for the rest of the year. We left in complete shock. That night we sat with my pastor and a few friends in almost total silence at the news. Together we prayed for the road ahead and that God would work wonders and healing in our lives. Each of us placed our lives into Jesus' hands knowing that He had it all under His sovereignty and control.

It was that night that set the stage for the next year of journeying a road I never imagined going down. It was a road of complete uncertainty and only in February of this year would I fully know the type of cancer I had and have a basic idea of what's ahead in the future.

In looking back over this past year I can only say that this journey, as hard and difficult as it was, was truly the best journey of my life thus far. I saw things in this world as I had never seen them before and I saw God at work like I had only seen in a very few people's lives. I literally saw the hand of God working in every aspect of my life. It was a true privilege to receive this calling from Jesus, and what a welcome companion He was in this trial and each day of my life.

Even though life was turned completely upside down, I have learned through this to truly live life. And though my life has been completely unexpected I am ever grateful for the life I currently have. The future remains completely unwritten and I'm gladly taking each day as it comes to whatever end the Lord wills.

We didn't know this a year ago, but I was diagnosed with brain cancer during Brain Cancer Awareness month. God has such a sense of humor!

SCRIPTURE INDEX

(Listed Alphabetically)

ACKNOWLEDGMENTS

To Jesus Christ – You answered my prayer when I desired Your will in my life; You knew exactly what I needed, when I needed it. What I needed was You, and You gave me the faith and hope to trust in You wherever You would take me in this world. You proved Yourself so faithful to me during this time and, truly, always. I welcome anything you may have in store, knowing Your presence will always be there. I long for the day that's to come to see You face to face, to sit down with You and talk. This life is all about You. Thank You for reminding me of that and for charging me to that glorious reality.

To Mom and Dad – You've been there for me every step of the way in this life. We've learned to make the best out of life, and the cancer was no exception. "Thank you," hardly explains the gratitude in my heart for you two.

To the courageous few – You each know who you are. You agreed to join the journey, not knowing where it would go; whether the end was healing or heaven, you were there. I'm ever grateful for your presence. I didn't ask you to come through the valley; you chose to. You showed me the love of Christ in your actions, your presence, and your prayers. You also showed me what the church is supposed to be, renewing my hope in the true body of Christ.

To Crossroads Community Church and Grace Baptist Church – You are my two church homes; one I grew up in, the other I helped establish. You were patient with all the prayer requests, faithful to pray, send notes of encouragement, and grow in Christ through the rejoicing and weeping of our lives. Crossroads, it's been a joy since the beginning and will continue to be a joy for the next hundred years. Stay faithful!

To the staff and students at the school where I teach – You've been a family to me, whether in providing meals or entertainment, knowing when to remove me from my classroom (even though I thought I could lie on my desk and teach), taking me to the hospital, subbing for me when I was having treatment, picking me up each morning to go to work when I couldn't drive, providing me the semblance of a normal life during the hardest days. You showed me that even though my life had stopped for a time, the world hadn't, and I needed to press on.

To Pastor Todd Smith – I remember the conversation we had the night I found out about the brain tumor, before the cancer diagnosis. You knew exactly what to say to set the stage for a path that would get significantly harder, showing me Christ and exhorting me to dwell on the truth of Christ. You were faithful beyond any expectations, and I am truly grateful for your presence and leadership throughout the entirety of the storm. I'm still working on memorizing Psalm 91, by the way.

To Dr. Liker, Dr. Bagga, Dr. Lai, Dr. Ellerbroek, and Dr. Schroeder – You and your amazing teams have profound gifts to provide the best medical care and support to your patients. We learned much through this, and I'm thankful you were each eager to grow as physicians through all the mystery of the cancer. You always treated me as a person—not a medical case—and were willing to do anything to restore my health.

To Michele Puglisi – You took my somewhat imperfect book and made it a little less imperfect with your insights, wisdom, and refinement. Thank you for investing the time to soften the rough edges.

To Brenda Strohbehn – You took my manuscript and made it even better in ways I never could. Your expertise, wisdom, and encouragement were just what my book and I needed.

To Mark Gooby – You are creative beyond my own abilities, and you took my ideas and made the perfect cover, with its depth and symbolism, beyond anything I could have imagined.

To the Quiet Warriors – So many of you, including many I do not personally know, committed to praying for me. Your silent presence through prayer and service did not go unnoticed. Thank you!

ABOUT THE AUTHOR

Adam Holland is a lifelong resident of Southern California, a founding member of Crossroads Community Church, and a history teacher at a local public high school. He earned his undergraduate and graduate degrees from The Master's College. *Anchored in the Storm: Pursuing Christ in the Midst of Life's Trials* comes out of Adam's battle with brain cancer and his desire to grow closer to Christ, and to see Christ at work through his own suffering and recovery.

CPSIA information can be obtained
at www.ICGtesting.com
Printed in the USA
FSOW01n0309221217
42659FS